# America Here I Come

*A Somali Refugee's Quest for Hope*

## Hamse Warfa

**Sunshine Publishing**
www.sunshinepublishingusa.com

Sunshine Publishing books may be purchased in bulk at special discounts for sale promotion, corporate gifts, fund-raising, or educational purposes. Special editions can also be created to specifications. For details, contact the Special Sales Department, Sunshine Publishing.

First Published 2014

Warfa, Hamse.
        America here I come : a Somali refugee's quest for
    hope / Hamse Warfa.
        pages cm
        Includes index.
        ISBN 978-0-9912819-0-9 (Paperback)
        ISBN 978-0-9912819-1-6 (PDF)
        ISBN 978-0-9912819-2-3 (EPUB)
        ISBN 978-0-9912819-3-0

        1. Warfa, Hamse.  2. Refugees--Somalia--Biography.
    3. Refugees--United States--Biography.    I. Title.

    HV640.5.S8W37 2014              305.893'54
                                    QBI14-600141

www.sunshinepublishingusa.com

# Praises for America Here I Come

"When David fought Goliath, he changed the rules and won. This same is true for Genghis Khan and most other winners. Adversity became the great asset. Hamse Warfa grabs this notion and throws his all into America. Read this. Your adversity may be your greatest strength."

> — *Duane Benson, trustee for the Minnesota State Colleges and Universities, former legislator, former NFL football player*

"Fascinating and informative for both immigrants and mainstream readers, Mr. Warfa's memoir is bound to inspire anyone. From a boy caught in a civil war to peacebuilder in the United States, this book is a testament to the strength of the human spirit."

> — *Judy A. Bernstein, co-author of "They Poured Fire On Us From the Sky"*

"I met Hamse while researching The Try, Jim Owen's book about the power of determination, and knew his story of courage and resilience had to be told. Hamse's own book delves deeper into his path from child refugee to global leader, offering unforgettable lessons to seekers and strivers everywhere."

> — *Marji Wilkens, Wilkens Communications*

"Hamse Warfa is an amazing man with an extraordinary story, and it is exceptionally well told. It is a model for anyone trying to adapt to a new life while remaining

committed to his original homeland and the people he loves."
> — *Charles F. (Chic) Dambach, Past President, Alliance for Peacebuilding*

"Hamse Warfa makes an important contribution to his adopted homeland by sharing the compelling story of his sojourn from East African refugee camps to management responsibilities at a Minnesota philanthropic foundation.

Readers will come away not only admiring the Warfa family, but also understanding better all the new immigrant communities that have sprung up in America in the last three decades – and are coming still."
> — *Lori Sturdevant, Editorial writer and columnist, StarTribune*

"Hamse presents some of the most difficult circumstances of his life in a way that helps us to see great things are possible with self confidence, faith and hard work. This book and Hamse's story is inspiring and encouraging and a great read for those who seek to be leaders in business or politics."
> — *Jeff Johnson Hennepin County Commissioner*

"Hamse Warfa's story is both interesting and important. Giving glimpses of Somalia few westerners get first hand, he not only tells of that trauma, but goes on to give outstanding advice about how anyone can succeed right here in the United States. America Here I Come is

exciting, challenging and makes a real contribution to its readers."
    — *Anne Wayman Author, blogger*

"I had the privilege to work with Hamse as a part of the San Diego Unified Schools Somali/District Task Force for four years. This book is a testimony to the "How come" he was able to be such a vibrant advocate for Somali students, parents, and community concerns. His trajectory into the mainstream public is of no surprise to me. His insights will assist the American public to become culturally proficient in living with one of our latest immigrant populations in the galaxy of star cultures that make America great."
    — *Agin Shaheed, Race Human Relations & Advocacy, San Diego Unified School District (SDUSD)*

"Hamse's story is inspiring and authentically American. If you ever find yourself lamenting America's standing in the world, crack open America Here I come to wash away your cynicism."
    — *Keith Ellison, Member of Congress*

"Flight from the Somalia Civil War to life in the refugee camps of Kenya is told through the childhood eyes of Hamse Warfa, a remarkably clever boy with a large family who bolster his efforts.

Hamse comes of age in Denver, CO, and in the inner city Heights in San Diego. He emmerges from his cocoon into a strong and resilient young man ready to confront the world as a leader in peacebuilding and with hopes for re-making his native country of Somalia while contributing significantly to his new home. Hamse's spirit and energy will be caught by all those who read this engaging book."

*— Senior Judge Lynn C. Olson, Minnesota District Court ESL certified Instructor and Director of Language Central, Inc, an adult language school teaching English to immigrants and refugees*

"As a University of Minnesota Regent, academic adviser and admissions officer, I have spent over a decade advo-cating for immigrant access to higher education. Hamse Warfa's story is an inspiring example for those who are committed to the success of our refugee youth."

*— Maureen Ramirez, Policy Director, Growth & Justice and Former University of Minnesota Regent*

Hamse writes clearly and honestly about surviving the war in Somalia. His book is a thoughtful introduction to Somali culture while at the same time providing an understanding of an immigrant's view of America. Everyone can gain from his insights about what comprises a true leader.

*— Anne Ehrhardt Wilbur, writer*

# Prologue

At first glimpse, the most astonishing thing about me might seem to be that I have the audacity to write this book. I am a refugee from Somalia, and my story represents the stories of many, not just those who have come to this country escaping horrible conditions at home, but also those who have overcome adversity and have made the decision to continually persevere.

By reading this book, you will not only learn about the traumatic and triumphant circumstances of my personal life, but more importantly, the book demonstrates how I overcame great obstacles and still keep pushing on to achieve a great end. In retrospect, all that happened could have easily crushed me and forced me to lose all hope and ambitions in life. Fortunately, faith in God, personal decisions I have made, love and guidance from family, friends and teachers have prevented me from letting circumstances dictate my life.

I was inspired to write this book when Jim Owen, the author of *The Try: Reclaiming the American Dream* (New York: Skyhorse Publishing, 2010) included my story in a dozen other true stories of ordinary people who've done extraordinary things.

Since the story was published, I have been contacted by countless people who said they found my story to be a source of inspiration.

I often tell my story in schools, non-profit centers, corporations, and other public gatherings; much to my amazement there is real demand for a book such as this. While my story is inspirational to immigrant youth who often don't have mentors, it is, amazingly, the mainstream population that is demanding to learn more about my life.

This book has thus been born out of the requests and encouragement of these amazing people. *America Here I come: A Somali Refugee's Quest for Hope* tells the narrative of my life in five parts. The first part of the book describes my early life in Somalia, my escape from the civil war and the challenges of life as a refugee in Kenya. The second part talks about an important turning point in my life: coming to America.

The book's third part discusses the place of immigrants in American society, while the fourth part relates to how I gradually began taking charge of my life and deciding the kind of destiny I wanted. The fifth and final part of this book discusses my understanding of leadership, and why I chose leadership development as my most important pursuit. There are also simple lessons that you can draw from my life's circumstances to help you turn your current challenges into opportunities for growth.

While reading through the five parts of the book, there are three main themes that the reader will find strongly emerging:

- Challenges might feel like threats towards progress in your professional and private life. However, by summoning your willpower to overcome, you create inner strength, which you can keep drawing upon whenever you face similar challenges. This is what makes you a consistent achiever.

- Continuous personal and professional development is key to personal growth and financial freedom. This is also an important means by which to achieve most of the goals you consider important in your life. Continuous learning gives you a helicopter view of things, and from up there you can easily identify opportunities and threats without getting entangled with the mess of immediate circumstances.

- Every circumstance in your private and professional life calls for leadership. And the world is asking: "Can we count on you?"

Finally, I have made many references to the armed conflict that the country of Somalia has suffered over the last twenty years. I was a victim of the war, and that is why my family and I came to the United States as refugees. My intention, however, is not to pass judgment over who was right or wrong. It's not the purpose of this book. I have done my best to stay away from politics, especially the politics of the violence that happened in Somalia. I have also steered clear of referring to people's clan identities or affiliations. This is because clanism has been a sensitive issue in Somalia, and I would wish to have this book viewed as a tool for peacebuilding and national healing.

I would like to once again thank you for your time to read this book. I pray that it will inspire positive change and will lead many more people, especially the youth, to become global ambassadors for peacebuilding and advocates for education.

# Contents

## Chapter 11

# Introduction

The hustle and bustle of modern-day America can be many. Like almost every other professional, I have to wake up before dawn and head to my home office to plan my day.

I check out my diary to see who I am supposed to meet, at what time and where. I check out too what the deliverables will be for me, and once again confirm that the objectives I set before going to sleep last night will be achievable before I call it a day later in the evening.

Satisfied that everything is on a good course, it's now time to step out of the office room and start helping two of my children: Samia, six-years-old, and Subeir, five-years-old, prepare for school. Sabrina, our one year-old lastborn, is in the meantime left at home with her mother, Ikran Abdi, who will later in the day be heading to class.

Ikran hopes to become a nurse in the not-so-distant future. This is a dream that I am doing my best to help her achieve—though I know I can never repay her for the sacrifices she has made for our kids and me. She is my best friend, my love, and the mother to my lovely kids.

At work, I know I will find the correspondence in my in-tray overflowing. Not that I am lazy—I have spent this entire week out of office in meetings. My day job is with Margaret A. Cargill Philanthropies (MACP), which serves as the umbrella over three grant-making organizations founded by the late Margaret A. Cargill, all with a common mission: To provide meaningful assistance and support to society, the arts and the environment. The philanthropies provide funding to organizations engaged in nonprofit work, both domestic and global.

In the evening I will be at the Institute for Horn of Africa Studies and Affairs (IHASA), a think tank that I helped establish in 2008 in a quest for lasting peace and development in the region. It is at this institute that I spend considerable amounts of time outside of my work with MACP. At IHASA, we are currently organizing for the annual academic conference. It is during such occasions that we bring together eminent scholars and community members to discuss socio-economic and political issues, and also train youth on leadership and conflict analysis in preparation for upcoming leadership roles. While the institute's members are predominantly Somali, we also have Kenyans, Ethiopians, and Sudanese, among other nationals whose countries have of late suffered armed conflicts.

IHASA has been attracting considerable international attention for the role it is playing in demystifying the conflicts in the Horn of Africa. We discuss the dynamics of the Darfur crisis and other conflicts in Sudan. There has been a perpetual border standoff between Ethiopia and Eritrea, piracy on the Somali Indian Ocean coast, as well as Ethiopia and Kenya's deployment of their military to Somalia. The list of conflicts is endless. One of our goals at IHASA is to analyze how these conflicts began and what must be done in their aftermath.

Since the return of relative peace in many parts of Somalia, thanks to diplomatic and military interventions by the UN and Africa Union among other bodies, there has been growing interest among Americans and Somalis to invest in the country. However, they need credible and independent assessments of the political situation and investment opportunities on the ground. That is also something we strive to provide at IHASA, through our network of socio-political and economic researchers and analysts both in Africa and here in the Diaspora.

So, I only got a chance to pass by my office last evening on my way home. A glance at my smart phone tells me my inbox is full. I try to imagine just how many people are competing for my time—and I have to heed most of them—given the urgency and nature of the services that they need from me.

Challenging as the nature of my work might seem, I feel this is completely in sync with my personal values and mission in life, which include providing leadership and creating opportunities for a better world through charity work. At MACP, I work closely with the organization's leadership on the development and implementation of large and small grant opportunities that will improve the conditions of local communities around the world.

On a typical day and outside of my work at the MACP, I might have an appointment to discuss an item or two

with the local congressman, give a talk on the importance of peace at a college, and still find time to sit with
my professor to thresh out a few details about the doctoral degree in Public Administration that I am currently
pursuing at Hamline University. However, all this isn't
supposed to get in the way of my passion—helping and
contributing my two cents to improve the lives of the
most vulnerable in our society, especially refugees.

I understand the plight of refugees, having been one
of them during perhaps one the worst of times in Africa.
This is after war broke out in Somalia in 1991, prompt-
ing my family to abandon all we had and embark on
a treacherous journey to the Dadaab Refugee camp in
the arid northeastern part of Kenya. We later moved to
Utange camp on the Kenyan coast, and then the Eastleigh section of Nairobi before coming over to the United
States as refugees.

I understand the meaning of deprivation, hunger, confusion and senseless loss of life. I, too, have experienced
the tragedy of waiting for help from officials of all kinds
who, despite the years of training in college, unfortunately never understood the meaning of these three simple words: "Emergency Humanitarian Assistance." As a
result of delayed responses, I have seen people's conditions—physical and psychological—deteriorate to the
point of leading to mental disorders and death under the
worst of circumstances. It is this kind of suffering that
pushed me to a career in humanitarian support.

My heart sinks each time I meet a child from a family
that has recently moved to the United States in an escape
from armed conflicts in some part of the world.

If you have never experienced war, let me give you a simple exposé of the kind of experience that you come across in this type of environment and that you are confronted with when you work with survivors of war and persecution. Think of the violence—not the kind we see in movies, but harrowing experiences such as a young boy of perhaps eleven or twelve seeing his kid sister fall out of his mom's arms, because his mom tried to dodge a bullet that unfortunately hit the sister. Then a second bullet shatters through the air and this one finds its original target—mom goes down as well!

Instinctively the boy ducks down and feigns lifelessness, sandwiched between the two writhing bodies of his mother and sister. He hopes and prays that they survive, though from the corner of his eyes he can see the heaving of his mom's chest getting weaker and weaker. The blood oozing from his mother's wound under the left arm forms a little stream. The boy sees the stream find its way towards him, like surface runoff when raindrops collect on the ground, seeking a downward-facing gradient to start the journey to the sea.

The stream finds its way to where the boy lies, less than a meter away from the mother. He hates this little and silent torture down here, but he dares not move lest he gets discovered and the gunmen come to finish him too. He can hear footsteps approaching, yet he dares not to check whose or from where. He had been taught that, in cases like these, he should lie still like a corpse until he is certain that the danger is over.

So he remains just there, eyes halfway closed, feigning lifelessness. Mom's blood reaches his forehead. He hates the feel of it, but still he dares not move. The blood forms a small pool around the left side of his head. He closes his eyes to mourn his dead mom and that little angel—his sister. It is the first time that the boy feels the pungent smell of human blood mixed with earth on a dusty village road.

"This one isn't dead!" says a male voice.

He can feel shadows crossing over him. Having held his breath for far too long, he is almost giving up now.

"If he isn't dead, he must be really suffering inside," says a second voice, more sympathetic and concerned.

The boy almost raises his head to greet the good Samaritans, but then he hears the sound of metallic shrieks. It's a rifle getting cocked.

"We shouldn't let someone suffer this much, it's totally inhuman."

"Oh! You almost shot at a corpse, see there's blood on the lower side of the boy's head," says the first voice.

"Lucky corpse! Thank goodness the cost of ammo is rising, just like the cost of food everywhere. Let's go."

The shadows cross over the boy's face again. There's sound of boots grinding against the road, and off the strangers go. But the boy remains just there, too afraid of the rapid transformations that have taken place in his life. Too afraid to die, but still even more afraid to live, if this is what life can be reduced to. Wanting to get up and run to safety, but he is too afraid of leaving his mom and sister's bodies behind. They are all he owns for now. The fact that his life and theirs has been brutally torn apart, for reasons he might never understand, seems to magnify their significance in his life even more.

Oblivious of the dangers lurking on this battlefield, he rises up, collects his little sister's body—careful not to press the lower abdomen where the bullet pierced her—and slowly rests the body next to his mother. There are renewed sounds of gunfire but they don't mean anything to him anymore. He leans forward, hugs the two bodies, cries and passes out.

So, this is the kind of trauma that the boy knocking at the door has gone through. He might never know what happened after he passed out, and the only friends he has are officers from the Red Cross. They are the only people who appear to understand him.

He can't understand why someone in his right senses would shoot at an innocent mother and kill an innocent girl barely four-years-old. Why on earth would a trained soldier take aim at innocent people and pull the trigger? Are wails of helpless people a thrill to the ears of the killers?

Out of his experiences, the poor boy now believes that bad things can just happen to anyone for no reason. If anyone can just pull the trigger and end someone's life for no reason, who will ever reassure the boy of his safety anywhere? How is the world expected to rebuild the boy's belief in himself, make him trust others, including armed cops?

With the incident so vivid in his mind as long as he lives, then how, unless someone really takes personal interest in the boy, will he ever be able to accept his past and pursue a purposeful future?

Despite all this, the boy is a hero. Since the war started in his country, the boy had stopped going to school, conquered hunger and inhumane treatment, survived a deprived childhood among other harsh conditions, and lived to tell the tale.

This happens to a boy at an age when a typical child in a peaceful land is beginning to explore in what subject to major in college, what career to pursue, what sports club to join, among other things. In a big way, as happened to me, war can change a child's sense of being and badly affect his understanding of the meaning and purpose of life.

Each refugee from war has a unique story to tell of escape from war. This is the same whether one comes from Darfur in Sudan, Goma in the Democratic Republic of Congo, Muyinga in Burundi, or, like me, Mogadishu in Somalia. Just like the boy in the story above, I once sought for purpose in life without an answer. I once bore his sorrows, walked his paths with sore feet, cried for help to a world that seemed indifferent, suffered the little boy's losses and lived through the confusion that once made life seem so unfair and meaningless.

Yet here I am, trying to write a book to create awareness and contribute my two cents worth. This is what I believe I was born to do. I can't figure out a way of life that doesn't involve putting a smile on a desperate face. Nobody said it was going to be an easy task, but someone has to ensure that the needs of vulnerable people are met.

By doing philanthropy, I am keenly aware of the fact that something needs to be fixed back where the refugees come from. There is need for permanent solutions to the causes of conflict in Africa and many others parts of the world. Otherwise, no amount of humanitarian assistance is ever sufficient to compensate for a world running away from its problems.

In a similar way, I can't pretend to have a solution to all the challenges that immigrants from Africa, or anywhere else, will ever face in their attempts to settle down to a new life here in the United States. I believe that the U.S. government, social service agencies and mainstream American society in general have already done a great deal in providing immigrants an opportunity to start life afresh. However, both host communities and immigrants need to reach out to each other, understand one another and explore how best to live as one equal and prosperous society; that has been the goal of American society since the foundations of this great nation.

As a member of the network of professionals and organizations attempting to make a difference in people's lives, I want to know each day that I have done my part, especially for immigrants. In doing this, I derive energy and strength from knowing that there is hope for each immigrant child and family to rise from their current circumstances and live a far better kind of life than they would perhaps have led if they had not emigrated.

Though the transformational process might not be as immediate as the people going through it would like it to be, it nonetheless has a definite outcome. I believe that the first stage of a bright and successful life here in America is that of securing a place in the classroom. That's what my dad always told me about education—it is the key to a bright future. I have tested the theory and found it to be true no matter what age one sets out to seek more knowledge and professional skills.

Certainly, I am not the most learned Somali in the world. I just happen to have a passion for education. Within the limited confines of my time here in America, I have experienced the transformational power of education. Having started off as a dish washer at a McDonald's restaurant in Denver, Colorado, today I work as a program officer with one of the largest philanthropies in the world. This is by no means the highest position an immigrant can reach. I just mention it here to help you see that if you seek out help that is available in this country, everything is possible as long as you believe in yourself and if you have the zeal to achieve.

For the new immigrants or those planning to come and make the United States their new home, be well aware of the following: You simply can't advance in your profession here without the necessary academic papers to prove your qualifications. Second, qualifications from most colleges and universities in third world countries are not recognized here. Therefore, if you hope to make it in your profession, be ready to start everything over from scratch—right from studying afresh for your degree or diploma. This is notwithstanding that you might have earlier taken a six-year degree course in medicine and surgery, engineering, or whatever your chosen line of profession may be.

Luckily, for those who came in as youngsters like I did, there are a thousand and one ways to advance in your chosen line of profession, provided you are willing to work hard and have the necessary financial support to pay for your education and training. Once again, I stress the key word "willing to work." This is because, unless you have the willpower to push on with your academic goals, there are enough temptations to make one want to opt out of the classroom and get to life in the fast lane, which usually does not pay off in the long run.

The majority of these temptations present themselves as quick solutions to the problem of lack of adequate finances to pay for your education. There are many promises of seemingly simple jobs to earn you large bucks, in some cases running errands for drug peddlers. While there is nothing wrong with working to finance your up keep and education, getting on the wrong side of the law is one of the worst things that an immigrant can ever do in the United States.

The consequences of spending life with hard-core criminals in a foreign jail or even deportation are undoubtedly too high a price to pay compared to walking the narrow and straight path to your goals in life.

# Part 1

# My life in Africa

# A Brief History of Somalia

The Republic of Somalia is located in the eastern part of Africa. Somalia forms the cap of the Horn of Africa, bordered by Kenya in the south, Ethiopia in the west, Djibouti in the northwest, the Gulf of Aden in the north and the Indian Ocean in the east. It is directly below and across from the Arabian Peninsula.

Historians argue that many of the recent conflicts in the region trace their origins to colonial powers drawing arbitrary boundaries across the land in disregard of indigenous people's way of life and aspirations. Somalia, one of the largest nations in Africa, sharing a common language, culture, religion and geographical area, was thus doled out among European colonizers, with each master to do as they pleased with their share of the land and human resources. The land was thus split into: British Somaliland, Italian Somaliland, and French Somaliland. In addition, Britain later transferred a large part of their colonial territories to King Menelik of Ethiopia, what is historically known as the Ogaden region. Britain was to then allocate another large expanse of Somali-inhabited territory land to Kenya; this now forms part of Kenya's northeastern province and was formerly known as the Northern Frontier District (NFD).

In the run up to the Somalia's independence in 1960, Italians put some effort in preparing the people in their territory for self-governance. This included training them on how to run the institutions of a parliamentary democracy, something that didn't happen, or wasn't effectively done in the other territories—the French, British, British Kenyan or in the Ethiopian areas. However, none of the colonizers had helped prepare Somalia for economic independence.

In the Somali Republic, which emerged when British and Italian Somaliland's decided to join, civilian administrations were followed by a military dictatorship (1969-1991). In good Cold War fashion, this dictatorship was supported and armed first by the Soviet Union and then by the U.S., without anyone caring much about the fate of ordinary Somalis. When the Cold War came to an end, and the two superpowers withdrew their support from the undemocratic regimes they had supported and maintained in power, many parts of Africa fell into civil war. This also happened in Somalia and is the background to my own flight from my native country.

As in Rwanda, where the Belgian colonial power emphasized ethnic divisions by issuing identity cards indicating an individual's ethnic (Hutu or Tutsi) identity, so in Somalia colonial administrations ruled their subjects as clans. This led to political competition between clans and, during the dictatorship, to a vicious and violent clan divide-and-rule policy. This became Somalia's Achilles' heel, and has remained the easiest handle through which Somalis have been misled and manipulated towards the selfish ends of most political leaders.

In 1977-1978, the nationalist desire for re-unification of the larger Somali nation led Somalia under President Mohamed Siad Barre into armed conflict with Ethiopia over the Ogaden region (also called Western Somalia), the inhabitants of this region are Somalis. This period also saw Somalia try to reclaim the Somali-inhabited territory from Kenya. In both instances, Somalia was defeated. Worse, these attempts saw Kenya and Ethiopia sign a mutual defense treaty to protect against future Somali attempts.

Without the support of the Organization of African Union, which had decided to uphold colonial boundaries, Somalia found itself politically isolated from its neighbors in East Africa. This isolation affected Somalia's economic development as well, thus drowning it in corrupting foreign aid and Cold War pay-offs.

Clamor for Barre's Ouster

Even though I did not know much about the war or what its cause was, I later came to learn that there were important factors that contributed to the downfall of Somalia's government.

To the outside world, Somalia represented one of the nation-states in Africa. It was a homogeneous community sharing a common language, culture and religion. So to many observers, it was hard to comprehend protracted armed conflict of the resulting magnitude within such a setting.

However, on the ground, agitations to rid Somalia of Siad Barre's rule had been long coming.

Indeed, historians say the collapse of the Somalia state

was in the offing right from independence. It was mainly on account of power struggles that pitted the three colonizers that colonized Somalia: Britain, Italy and France. This was back in the period between 1940 and 1946, when each of the colonizers had a swath of land under their control.

In 1946, Ernest Bevin, then British foreign minister, came up with a plan to unite the whole of Somalia, which was previously under three colonial masters, but this plan flopped as each of the masters stood to benefit more from a divided as opposed to a united Somalia.

Although British Somaliland was declared independent on June 26, 1960, and Italian Somaliland on the first of July the same year, with the two joining hands to form the Republic of Somalia, the differences in perspectives and opposing interests in the two regions became important causes of frequent disagreements for the two sides, despite the years that had passed since independence. The region under France went ahead to become the republic of Djibouti later in 1977.

For keen observers, signs of impending eruptions of violence were written all over the wall since 1977, when Siad Barre deployed the Somali Army to capture the Ogaden territory from Ethiopia. This was the second attempt after an earlier one had failed in 1963. Even though the Somali army captured most of the Ogaden this time around, as the country had one of the best armies in Africa at the time, it was nonetheless repulsed after Ethiopia got support from the Soviet Union and Cuba, which sent thousands of troops to prop up Ethiopia.

With the retreat, and having spent considerable

amounts of resources in the misadventure, Somalia was limping economically, politically and now militarily. The levels of demoralization and mistrust among soldiers started becoming issues of serious concern, and the threat of splitting up the military along separate loyalties became even more pronounced.

Despite having been a great crusader for putting an end to clan-based politics in the country, Barre returned to this old tactic to survive through this period when people's support for the government was at an all-time low.

But the resulting divide-and-rule scheme that he deployed against the various Somali clans was evidently only going to last for as long as the people were willing to tolerate it. And it didn't take long for the people's anger towards the government to boil over.

Though young, I often heard stories of torture and strong opposition to dissent. For instance, I remember hearing how the government security forces had direct permission from the highest office in the land to use torture and humiliation in weeding out dissenting forces across the country. I recall, too, hearing of the execution of hundreds of demonstrators who were protesting the arbitrary arrest of their spiritual leader. This had been carried out by the Red Berets, the government's anti-reprisal special unit.

Such callous activities specifically targeted at peaceful dissent destroyed any remaining legitimacy and tarnished the government's image domestically and globally. By now, many different armed opposition groups had formed to topple the government.

I still recall my brothers, uncles and neighbors engaging in thorough analysis of the strengths and weaknesses of each of these factions and debating whether they could actually succeed in their mission. There were questions too of who was sponsoring the factions, as well as the objectives of the sponsors.

The local analysts talked of diminishing morale within the Somali Army, especially after its defeat in the Ogaden war, a factor that was now rendering the national army less effective in combating the opposition. There was the clan factor too in Somali's political landscape that had been demanding allegiance and support from the national army commanders.

There had been growing dissent of Barre's twenty years of Supreme Revolutionary Council (SRC) rule, especially coming from clans hitherto thought to be loyal to the government.

This was more so, after the failed coup attempt on Barre's government in April 1978, engineered by Colonel Mahammad Shaykh Usmaan. As a result, the Colonel and sixteen fellow coup leaders had been summarily executed for their roles in the failed coup.

Though I had learned about these and many such occurrences, what I was missing was the context. How would all that affect me? Why did my family and I have to worry about people who carried guns? I didn't know anything about repression, lack of democratic space or even freedom of association.

I didn't know about civil liberties and that lack of them was what was fuelling reprisals across the entire country.

I recalled, for instance, the story of my cousin Abdirashid who has been missing to this day after being drafted for the Ogaden war. Stories had it that he was a tall, handsome and strong man full of care and compassion. Abdirashid did well in school before he was drafted into the army and sent to fight. He never came back, and to this day no one bothered to explain to his family what had befallen him.

Though the agitations succeeded in rooting out Barre in 1991, they nonetheless failed to fill the power vacuum that resulted. As such, different armed groups took over governorship of different regions of the country. Civilians were deliberately targeted because of their clan affiliation. Power struggles arising from these illegitimate clan-based leaderships resulted in the country's worst and one of Africa's longest armed conflicts.

# Chapter 1
# Childhood in Mogadishu

In the 1980s, Somalia was at peace and life was good. There were a million things to occupy a boy's day in Mogadishu. My day would start early in the morning. Our family was large; fourteen and I was number twelve, with only two siblings younger than me.

Mohamed Warfa Magan, my dad, left for work at 5:30 every morning. His favorite outfit was a well-cut grey suit (it so happens that grey suits are my favorite too). My father was a businessman engaged in the import and export trade. He always told me of his life struggles— the difficult childhood he had suffered, and how it had made him who he now was. At a young age, he had fled from the Somalia-Ethiopia conflict over the disputed Ogaden territory. This meant he had been forced to walk for months to reach Somalia. Sadly, this was a fate that would later befall me in my teenage years, whereby I would find myself in a confused haze escaping the burning city of Mogadishu, heading to a refugee camp hundreds of miles away in Kenya.

With no money, support or place to turn, my father had to seek refuge at a mosque where he knew no one. This helped him develop people skills that would serve him well later as an entrepreneur. After a few months, he secured a job with a trader who exported livestock to the Middle East and other parts of the Horn of Africa region. My father worked for this trader for several years until he had saved enough to start his own business as a livestock trader. Later on, my father met my loving and beautiful mother, Hindisa Hassan Seed. With my mother's support and encouragement, my father's company grew steadily to become a large livestock trading company. This is where my family's business success started.

If there is something that I and everyone else at home remember our dad for, it was his emphasis on education as the key to a successful life. Though he didn't have the pleasure to study much himself, he was candid that time had changed and that the economic fortunes of his generation wouldn't be of much use to us unless we went to school and worked hard and became what each one of us wanted to be in life. He thus ensured that we all attained the highest quality of education possible. He also helped my mother establish a successful clothing retail business in Mogadishu, which she ran for 25 years until the war broke out in 1991.

Before the war, I honestly hadn't known the meaning of deprivation. I might not have had the trendiest toys while growing up, but at least we had what we needed to feel loved and cared for by our parents.

On the account of Dad's flourishing import and export business and Mom's retail store in the city, my family lived quite comfortably in an affluent part of Mogadishu. More walkways were paved than in other parts of the city, and driveways in our neighborhood were some of the best, something that, by third world standards at that time, was something to write about. Our house sat on a large compound, structured like the single-family homes built in the United States in the 1980s. It was a single-story building with eight rooms.

As early as the age of five, word has it that I had identified blue as my favorite color. I had even requested my parents to have the walls of the room that I shared with my brothers painted blue. Although this might not have been an ideal color to match our home, which was tan-colored on the outside, my parents had accommodated my request. Wali, my elder brother, often explained to me that, as a child, I should let my parents decide certain things, as they knew more than me and their choices were informed by wider considerations than I might have understood. As I grew, so did my personality, and even more so, my curiosity.

I questioned everything. I wanted to know why we ate rice and fish so often, why dad woke up so early and where he was going, why my elder brothers and sisters wore white shirts and khaki pants to school, and why we had to go to school every working day. In a home that sheltered more than twenty people, my questions were as limitless as the responses I received.

My brothers and sisters lived with us until they got married and went to start their own families. Others, including my cousins, traveled to other places to seek higher education and employment.

Before leaving home for work each morning, Dad dutifully woke us up to prepare for school. That would signal the start of our daily scramble. The toilet is busy.

The shower is occupied. Now who took my clothes from here, this is where I left them! The teacher will mark you as late if you don't come in on time, and there would be punishment for that. The transportation van is hooting outside. With little time for breakfast, we often left cups halfway full with tea on the table—much like satisfied kids at a party. Only that this time we left with rumbling bellies, longing for the day to end so we could return home and get a proper meal.

I attended Hussein Giire elementary school, while Abdirizak and Abdullahi, two of my elder brothers, as well as Fardowsa and Nasra, two of my elder sisters, went to Banadir Baarbe High School.

School was fantastic for me! My brother, Abdirizak, tells me that the educational quality of my school was superior, as we had top of the range teachers. My Somali and Arabic teachers were great and had made me fall in love with the subjects.

Learning was made even more fun by the academic rivalry that I later came to learn was specifically designed by the teachers to motivate us. Within my grade, which had four separate streams, the constant inter-class competitions in various academic disciplines brought forth selected pupils who would represent the school in annual inter-school competitions.

Equally, inter-school drama, Somali literature and sports competitions were events to look forward to. Each district would hold preliminaries, during which schools in our northern district would go head-to-head in selected areas of competition. This would bring out the best talents in the various grades from the participating schools. These would then represent the district in the provincial competitions.

Our school's setting was amazing. It was in the middle of suburb of Medina, a neighborhood considered upscale considering the standards of some other neighborhoods. This was the school that kids of some of the most prominent people in Somalia attended, including the children of several generals in the national armed forces, ministers and prominent business people.

In Somalia, which was a Muslim country, Fridays were days to rest and attend prayers. This meant that unlike most of the western world, in Somalia the week started, and still starts, on Saturday. Thursdays served as schools' sports days, and there were no excuses for not attending. Students with physical disabilities were especially encouraged to join in the sporting fun.

Of all games, soccer was the most popular. This was because, besides giving all of us an equal opportunity to run around and display our antics, assembling at the field had a different purpose. It provided an arena for girls to show off their beauty, at least within the limits that the school uniform of white, short-sleeved shirts and khaki skirts would allow.

School life was amazing. Beyond the classroom activities, sport competitions, drama events and field excursions were things to look forward to. Twice a year school would organize field trips to places like Baidoa, Marka, Shalanbood and Jannaale--towns outside of the capital city. Students would go to the Sambusi Beach for a long weekend; fully organized and sponsored by the school. Or they would go to the citrus orchards at Shalanbood along the Shabelle River. This was unique opportunity to network, socialize and get to know each other.

There would be planned activities. Responsibilities given to students included marshaling, preparation of sleeping quarters, preparation of food, and organizing extra-curricular activities. Students would swim in the open ocean, run half a marathon, visit the local army training facility or dance to Somali music until the wee hours of the morning.

When out of school, life in Mogadishu was memorable in many ways. On any given afternoon, after lunch and brief nap, one would dress up to go to the city. Along the paved roads were cafes and restaurants.

Locals spent considerable time sipping sweet tea, listening to tales of bygone eras from the elderly, playing boqoliyo bun—a domino game—and card games called scallo and daba-ka-eri.

Boqoliyo bun loosely translates into "one hundred and one." It refers to the number of points the winning team garners. It is played by two pairs of contestants. The losing pair pays for the round of sweet tea and is replaced by another pair. The rivalry could continue for months.

Being a boy still at school, my days would be different, though. Early afternoon would see me go to an Arabic language School. I would later go to a private after-school program where students were helped with homework, especially on school subjects that one needed to excel in.

Mr. Dhakalow was a lecturer of Mathematics at the Somali National University. He was the main teacher at these afternoon private classes. Only serious students whose parents could afford to pay for the extra lessons attended.

During school holidays, afternoons also saw me spend hours playing soccer with my friends. There was serious rivalry between the boys in the area. I was a skilled soccer player and could run an opponent until he was tired. Mohamed-Ghani was the best in our group. He was an outstanding player. Among the friends we played with were Abdi Haji and his brother Mohamed Haji, Omar China, Saeed Leandro and others.

It later turned out, Abdi and Mohamed Haji's absent father was the leader of the Western Somali Liberation Front. This was a movement that was fighting to liberate the Somali region from Ethiopia and reunite it with Somalia.

After sunset, I would attend the evening prayers at the Masjid (mosque). Some days I would attend Qur'an translation and commentary classes. Other days I would be expected to assist my brothers and sisters in our family garden.

Although I was not old enough to experience it, I heard tales that night life in Mogadishu was especially great. Some nights there would be a play or a concert. Waberi, the Somali national band, was an especially popular group to go see. In any given week, there would be an outstanding Somali play in one of Mogadishu's theatres.

Besides Waberi there were the music and theater groups Iftin (for the Ministry of Education), Halgan (for the Army), Durdur (mainly for plays in the musical style of the Banadiri culture which had split off from Waberi) and many others.

One had the opportunity and choice to choose what type of play he or she attended. Traditional Somali plays such as "Waa maadays adduunyadu, dadkuna way matalayaan" ("The world is a play and people are [simply] actors in it") composed by Sangub (one of Somali's greatest poets and playwrights) are classical pieces that could rival Shakespeare's *Hamlet*. I have the audacity to claim that Somali poetry is second to none.

One had an array of stand-up comedians to choose from. These would cover anything from local politics, religion, Somali customs, to social norms and foreign matters. The nights at the concerts were not my favorites! I was too young to be out that late. But on some rare occasions my cousins would take me along and I would get a chance to recount the full episode to my classmate on the next school day.

In far greater numbers were the movie houses. We had cinemas that specialized in action movies, some in romantic movies and special ones for only Hindi movies. I was a big fan of cinema. Many times, I would go to the movie house and stay on until the end of the last show.

There were often two movies screened every night in Mogadishu theatres. The first show would start after sunset followed immediately by another. For the benefit of latecomers, the first movie would be repeated later at night. Life was very good for me: filled with school, friends, beautiful girl classmates, soccer, theatrical plays, movies and fun at the beaches. Some of the days were eventful in other ways though.

I will never forget the day my friend Ali and I went with my cousins to Lido beach. Right in the old section of

Mogadishu, Lido is home to many foreign-owned restaurants and cafés. We spent the day swimming in the ocean with no regard to time or place. Once we were done, my friend Ali and I went up to the showers along the beach, which were, unknown to us, reserved for tourists. While we were splashing in the cool salty ocean waters, an aggressive guard came along. He hurled insults at us. We ran away frightened.

My friend Ali, known for his bravery and cunning at times, would not let this unwarranted aggression go unanswered. He urged me to come along with him. We were tiny little boys but he wanted us to fight the mighty security guard. He could not understand why foreign tourists were allowed to bathe and shower but not us. I agreed with him fully.

So Ali went back into the water intentionally.

I sat on the edge clutching our bag. My instruction was to guard Ali against more security guys joining the fight. Ali was convinced he was capable of beating the heck out of this "ignoble" guard who was preventing us from enjoying what we believed belonged to us.

What ensued was both spectacular, from our point of view, and silly. The guard, incensed by the daring of this little boy, rolled up his sleeves and charged at Ali. Watching the guard's movement at the corner of his eye, Ali out-maneuvered the guard, tripped him on the wet floor and punched him on the nose and face in quick succession.

As we might have expected, an army of guards and business people descended on us. I pulled out a small baseball-like bat and tried to scare the men. Boy! Was I wrong! We were beaten so badly that we could not move a limb. Worse still, we were arrested and taken to the guards' center for further discipline!

But unbeknown to us as kids, the quality of life that we enjoyed is about to unravel.

# Chapter 2
## Escape from Hell

Y ou can never know what it feels like to be truly safe until you have run and dodged a storm of bullets flying around your head, looking for any kind of shelter, desperately trying to stay alive. If you can do this and make it through without a scratch, well then you will know the true meaning of safety.

I was twelve-years-old when war broke out in Somalia in 1991. Given president Siyad Barre's apparent firm grip on issues, few people thought anything major would come out of the agitations from across the country to oust the government. Otherwise, how did the opposition hope to get rid of a tyrant who had ruled the country for close to twenty years? What repression technique didn't he know and couldn't he use to grind down the opposition? After all, Barre's government had won itself the reputation of training its guns even on civilians.

But this time things were moving very fast. The propaganda machines on both sides, that of the government and that of the armed opposition groups were hard at work, with each side doing its best to whip up public emotions against the opponent. Thus, it didn't take long for either side to play dirty, if only to reassure the public which side was in control of power in Mogadishu. The dirtiest of all tricks was whipping up negative clan sentiments.

Strong affiliation to clan identity had all along been the weakest link in Somali's national fabric. Earlier on, the government had invested much to help galvanize the nation into a single community, regardless of one's clan affiliation. These plans proved insincere because Barre's government discriminated against certain clans it suspected of being in the opposition. As a strategy to remain in power and preventing unified resistance to his rule, Barre played a devious game of clan divide-and-rule, increasing distrust and hatred between groups.

Fanning clan sentiments was thus guaranteed to tear the nation down its seams, something that was sure to take ages to mend.

In the context of political instability and armed uprisings throughout the country, people became vulnerable to divisive political clan propaganda. As children, we went from peacefully playing soccer at school and in the neighborhood to suddenly realizing that we belonged to different clans. Though we couldn't tell what the differences between clan X and clan Y were, mainly because we had been born and brought up in urban centers, propaganda machines were right there on the ground to "educate" the children of their differences.

To the majority of us children, this did not make much sense. This was the saddest thing I had experienced so far. But feeling sad didn't stop things from deteriorating further. In a matter of days the mutual suspicion among different clans was rife to the extent of identifying who belonged to which clan and supported the government or the opposition.

It was becoming increasingly difficult to trust others. This meant it was difficult even for businesses to continue. There were talks of some business people refusing to sell essential goods and food to people from different clans. It all felt like a bad dream since no one could tell where things were headed or when the dawn would come, so we could put all this behind us and proceed with life as we were used to.

As the tensions grew, we watched our supplies of life's essentials dwindle. There was no more rice or spaghetti in the shops, and there were no more trucks bringing bananas to the city from the countryside. There was no more sugar in the shops, and on the few occasions when little supplies would come, it rarely reached the store. People would scramble over it, to the extent where the spilt quantities exceeded what anyone ever took home.

Soon, news of hijacking of vehicles carrying food supplies to other parts of Mogadishu and upcountry became the norm, as there was practically nothing for the people to survive on. Then there came rumors that the city water reservoirs had been poisoned. This was the scariest of all news, and you didn't dare test on yourself whether it was true or just a hoax. In a short period, Mogadishu city began grinding to its death.

This was the misery before the war actually got to the entire city. Just as we were getting accustomed to the life of scarcity, word came that the warring factions were gradually closing in on neighborhoods, including Medina where we lived. We soon began hearing sounds of gunfire and artillery almost on a daily basis, especially in the evenings. This was especially horrifying to innocent kids like us, who knew nothing about why there was fighting in the first place.

I will forever recall the day the war became personal to me. It was a Sunday in December, and the day began like most other school days. I was dressed up in my yellow shirt and khaki pants, heading to school. School was the only place where we could congregate, learn and play as if nothing strange was going on around us. For some reasons, we kept going to school even after most of the other life processes had grounded to a halt.

As it would happen once in a while, I would walk to school in the company of my elder brothers and sisters. On this day, my brother and I were walking with Yusuf, one of my best friends, and Kamal, the tallest kid in our class.

Unknown to me, those were going to be our last moments together. As soon as we had gotten through the school gates and each headed to their respective classrooms, word came round that government and opposition fighters were closing in on our neighborhood. We all took to our heels. Some of us jumped over the school's fence, while others had the courage to try their luck going through the regular gate. But we were scared stiff, and no one had the guts to wait and see what soldiers at war looked like. Each one of us headed wherever we thought safest—home.

Like most of us, Kamal ran back home to find his parents and siblings waiting for him so they could flee Mogadishu. Kamal was the only remaining member of the family before they all boarded a truck headed for Marka, a city in the Lower Shebelle region, which is about 68 miles Southwest of Mogadishu. So down the road the truck roared, with all the family members glad to have left the chaos of the fast encroaching war behind in Mogadishu.

Upon exiting from Mogadishu, the truck joined a convoy of about nine other trucks whose occupants were also heading to Marka to escape the city's impending destruction. But barely an hour into the journey, the most unexpected happened. Unbeknown to the drivers and everyone else in the convoy, the route they had taken ran through a battlefield. The convoy thus drove right into what seemed like a snare. They were hit with mortars from left and right. All nine of the trucks caught fire and just a handful of the people survived the midday attack. Kamal was not one of the survivors.

Yusuf had been lucky to get home safely. By evening that day, fighting had subsided considerably, and everyone was hopeful that the peace would hold. However, things had not been so good in Yaaqshid district of Mogadishu where Yusuf's sisters lived. Fighting there that had begun as armed conflict between government and opposition fighters had apparently turned into attacks by civilians of certain clans, now armed with any weapon they could lay their hands on, against members of other clans.

Yusuf and two of his brothers headed to Yaaqshid to evacuate his sisters, in response to a distress call. As fate would have it, they ran right into a gang of fighters associated with the opposition. It is said the fighters either suspected teenage Yusuf and his brothers were spies for the government forces or were killed because of clan af- fiiation. After brief interrogations, they were executed in cold blood. Later, the sisters managed to leave the dis- trict after an ultimatum was issued by a rival dominant clan that all people who did not belong to the clan should leave the area within twelve hours. My friends—Kamal and Yusuf—met their deaths long before they had even experienced the highs and lows of being teenagers.

I had never been so grief-stricken in my life. Now the reality of war was beginning to dawn on me. I still recall my elder brothers going to collect the bodies of Yusuf and his two brothers the following morning and taking them for burial at the local cemetery.

Somehow, I felt lost as to whether what my brothers were doing was right or wrong. I felt as if they had taken part in robbing me of such a close friend; yet, even at this age I knew duty had to be done and my brothers were just as grief-stricken as I to carry such close fam- ily friends to the grave that young. I felt I should have been there to meet whatever fate Yusuf might have faced. I still recall my sisters' acts of kindness, taking water to Yusuf's home and attending to the many mourners who visited to console the family.

## Hope and Procrastination

As the tension mounted, many of our neighbors kept boarding trucks with all their belongings, saying good- bye to Medina district of Mogadishu. They seemed certain that the war would soon engulf the city from all sides, and feared there would be no escape. But my family stayed put a little longer. Dad strongly believed the war would end before getting to our district. He was convinced too that there would be military intervention by other African states and the wider international community before Mogadishu exploded. Oh how mistaken he was!

Even as war began knocking at the gates of Medina, even as schools, businesses and markets closed, my family was still somehow not convinced that leaving the city was the wisest decision. So the deliberations went on:

Dad: "This isn't a large scale war. The situation will soon be put under control."

Brother Wali: "But why would we want to take the risk of staying put when we can safely escape from this hell, and return when things have calmed down?"

Dad: "But where do we go and where will we find guaranteed refuge?"

Wali: "The benefits of fleeing by far outweigh the risk of staying. We would rather look for a safer place while fleeing, than remain here and be engulfed by violence from all sides."

Dad (laughing): "Listen to my young sons and Hindisa (my mom). I have lived long enough and have developed analytical skills. I perfectly understand the kind of situation we are in. This is not the beginning of a war, but rather an uprising that will be quelled soon. The government will realize that it needs to open up the political space and also improve its people's conditions."

"We cannot take the risk of fleeing when we don't have enough money, we have no clue of where we are going and we may not even make it to safety. Why don't we calm down and stay in our house and assess the situation day by day?"

Mom: "I see both sides of the argument, but news coming from Yaaqshid and Wardhiigley is very terrifying. This is no longer a war of soldiers but a war in which innocent people like us are being targeted and terrorized. We are not sleeping at all from sounds of the artillery. I don't think we can risk staying here, especially with the children. We need to find safety, wherever that might be, and pretty fast!"

The debates went on. Personally I wanted to remain longer in Mogadishu; it is where I had such good friendships, so I kept praying for peace. However, the decision to flee finally got Dad's stamp of approval when the unexpected happened.

It was one quiet evening, around eight thirty. We had gathered as a family to eat and discuss the situation. Suddenly, there was a terrifying sound, which was followed by the loudest blast I have ever heard in my life. Flames illuminated every corner of our house. The light was so bright that it shone through the heavy drapes on the room's windows. The curtain box on the window overlooking the side of the blast fell off the wall.

The whole room felt like a vacuum or a compressed air chamber. As the drapes went down with the curtain boxes, I saw the glass windows bulge inwards, shatter and spew glass pieces all over the room. We ducked for cover under the furniture. Deafening silence followed. No one gathered the courage to utter a word for close to five minutes. Those few minutes seemed like the longest moments of my life. We just listened for any more sounds or movements from under the furniture, but everything was dead silent. We knew something terrible had happened, but no one could tell what it was. Still gasping for breath, we began to crawl out of our hideouts.

Mom was the first to talk, though in a hushed tone. "We are safe. God has spared us, my children. We weren't the target."

We crawled from under the tables and peered outside the window. It was Ifrah's home, poor little girl! The rebels had targeted and hit the dining room with precision, perhaps hoping to get Ifrah's dad, who was a general in Siyad Barre's government. The general survived, together with five other house occupants. Unfortunately, little Ifrah, her mother and two brothers who had been at the dining room at that moment were crushed beyond recognition. Their bodies were discovered a day later by fellow neighbors under the smoldering debris.

The compound on which the beautiful one-story mansion had once stood resembled a rubble dumpsite, with some of the concrete breaking the fence and flowing over to our side. Ifrah's home continued burning throughout the night. The neighbors were afraid of stepping in to help for fear of further attacks. I had never felt so exposed and vulnerable in my life. I had witnessed the callous nature of war, its insensitivity too, and I desperately felt that the war had to be stopped at whatever cost.

I had so far lost three close friends: Kamal, Yusuf and now little Ifrah in just a matter of days. The fighters had hit quite close to our home, and I was now convinced that neither the general nor our dad was immune to the attacks. I started getting this strange and desperate feeling that I too was a target—though I couldn't explain really why. I felt that the fighters were hell-bent on killing children and I was afraid that things were getting out of hand. I desperately wanted to do something, anything that could help end this senseless exchange of fire.

About six o'clock the morning after the blast at Ifrah's, community elders and local religious leaders held a brief meeting and informed us of their resolution. They too sensed the danger and felt there was need to sensitize the warring parties of the impact that their activities were having on us.

The leaders wanted us to organize a demonstration that would walk right into the heart of the war zone and tell the fighters to stop the war. To me, at least, this made sense. I wanted to look at the soldiers in the face and explain to them just how cruel they were by killing innocent children. I wanted to ask them what they had so far gained by killing Kamal, Yusuf and little Ifrah, and what they would gain by massacring more innocent kids.

After morning prayers at home, I ventured outside to see if my friends had heeded to the call. And there they were, about twenty youths from the neighborhood. What impressed me most were the inscriptions on the placards that they carried: "Peace," "stop the war," "innocent people are dying," "save Somalia from destruction." This resonated perfectly with what was in my heart and mind. They waved at me to join them and I did so, without any hesitation. Afterwards, we set off on our journey to the center of the city.

We walked towards the city chanting peace slogans. I really believed that we could stop the war if we made the best use of the opportunity we had for now. I however kept wondering why grownups weren't doing anything about the war, other than discussing in low tones how to run away from the city. Personally, I didn't have any idea of where we could possibly escape to. The only place I knew was the Medina neighborhood in Mogadishu, and I was prepared to do whatever it took to see peace restored in the city. I would later realize that my naiveté hindered me from fully understanding the consequences of the war.

Along the way we took time to explain our mission to bystanders. We explained to them that the city was ours, and it would therefore be wiser to stay put and defend the peace, than do the cowardly act of running away. "Things get worse when good people do nothing about bad situations," I recall one particular young man reasoning out with an elderly man in his late fifties. "You're right my son, take the message to the generals," he responded.

Everyone we talked to urged us on. The thought of being caught up in the armed conflict had terrified everyone, and people prayed for a miracle to happen and forestall the advancing fighters. I, however, could see the idea of joining our course scared the hell out of the youths we requested to join us along the way. The majority of them said they would join us in our second mission, because we hadn't informed them ahead of time so they would make the necessary preparations. I knew these were excuses to avoid joining us, but so what? We proceeded.

Because of the various stops we made along the way, it was about 2:00 p.m. when we entered Mogadishu's central business district. Our chanting hit a crescendo when we noticed the attention we got from the soldiers we passed along the way. We asked them to spare some time to go see how their families were faring on at home.

We asked them to demonstrate patriotism for once and stop the war. We challenged them to press their commanders that the cost of the war and its consequences would be a price too heavy to pay for Somalia, and that political differences would be best be settled at a round table, not in street fights or guerilla wars in the bush. But the soldiers just smiled and told us to return home.

"Who sent you here, and why would he not bring the message himself if he is genuine in his intentions?" Asked one of the soldiers we encountered in a group of four. He looked quite young and harmless for this kind of profession. He was slightly shorter than his three colleagues, and his slim frame wrapped in the jungle fatigue made him look like a new recruit into the forces. Unlike his colleagues, I noticed he hadn't steadied his gun when he saw us.

"It is our love for Somalia that has sent us here. And it is the genuineness of our intentions that has brought us this far. We want to ask the generals to end this war so that we can return to school and our parents and neighbors can get back to their work," said Hassan, one of the boys in our team.

"You have now demonstrated your love and patriotism for Somalia. Remember that Somalia is you, young boys, and the only way to keep Somalia safe is by ensuring you are safe. So, now just return home. We will tell the generals that you were here and you want the fighting to cease," the young soldier implored us.

But we didn't turn back; we marched on past the four soldiers. We wanted to take the message to the war generals and commanders—that had been our mission from the start and we weren't going to stop before we were done. We were harmless boys, after all. On we marched.

Suddenly we heard a gunshot that made us freeze. It had been fired at close range ahead of us, but we couldn't see anyone. From the shot's decaying sound I realized that it hadn't hit anything. We didn't know whether to proceed or to turn back and run.

"Don't run or else the soldiers shooting in the air will think we have ill motives. Come on, don't show cowardice. If we don't run, the soldiers will give us a hearing, and since ours is a peaceful mission, the soldiers will help us see their generals," rationalized Hassan. So we didn't disperse, though our bellies had melted to feel like half-filled tanks of water.

We summoned our courage and moved on, albeit with our knees shaking in fear. Suddenly there was a second sound of gunfire, followed by so many more that I lost count. Unlike the earlier shots that tore the air without hitting at a target, now the sounds were like quick short bursts of fire. I have never been so terrified in my life. Surprisingly, there were gunshots coming from behind us too, and there was no time to look back to check out the source.

Things were happening too fast. I saw someone squat with arms clutched at his abdomen, right there beside me. This is when I discovered that Hassan had just covered his face with his hands, sat down and resigned himself to fate. Something inside told me to run. I had learned a while back that moving targets are hard to hit with a bullet. As I jumped over Hassan, I stumbled upon someone else writhing in pain on the ground—I didn't know who it was. Then I saw a boy fall on his back with blood gushing from his neck. I can't recall what happened next; all I remember is taking to my heels, stumbling, falling, rising up and running away from the gun fire madness, unsure of where I was headed.

The popping sounds of the guns intensified and an occasional deathly scream from someone not so far away rent the air. I ran past the four soldiers we had seen earlier. They were all, including the seemingly harmless soldier, firing at the boys I had left behind. All I could hear now were "pop pop" sounds and desperate screams behind. I kept running.

I felt something like a huge bee pass by my left ear, and another one overhead. I ducked, feeling hot all over my body. I couldn't believe someone wanted me dead too, young and harmless as I was. I almost resigned to fate but instinct propelled me to keep running. I ran on to wherever my feet took me—there wasn't any decision to make now—just running and praying that God would help me out of the crossfire. I tripped and cursed as I hit some dirty soggy waters and lay prostrate on the ground. "This is my end—this is where I leave this world," I thought to myself.

I remained hunkered down for about three minutes. The gunfire died out. I tried moving my legs and thankfully they were still intact. I felt a sharp pain in my left ankle. I pulled up my leg to take a look, but there wasn't any blood. I was lucky to have escaped with a sprain and without a bullet. I was still alive, but with no idea of where I was or the next course of action.

Painful as the sprain was, I didn't know where medical assistance could come from. I didn't know where I was, so how could I know where to find a hospital? My teeth clenched with pain. I wiped sweat from my brow, and that is when I noticed that my heart was threatening to break out of my chest. I opened my mouth to catch some breath.

As I lay there, I recalled stories my cousin, Mohamed Hassan, had told my brothers, sisters and me. He had warned us that there were acts of compassion in battlefields, whereby soldiers would kill a badly wounded victim of war to end his agony. I feared that if I showed movement someone would feel obliged to shoot me to stop my suffering. This thought sent a shiver down my spine. Had I escaped a shootout just to come and surrender my life to the so called act of benevolence? No way! I had to get out of the city and run back home.

I opened my eyes and peered into the sky. It was still blue. I looked at the buildings around me, trying to get my bearing. That's when I realized how buildings can resemble each other from the worm's eye view. This was a ghost city. The gun sounds had died off. There was hardly any movement, despite it being a time when ordinarily the streets of Mogadishu would be bursting with people.

I wanted to get up and start finding my way home, but the thought of running into soldiers made me shudder and lie prostrate. I remained rooted there, knowing what I was supposed to do, but too frightened to dare move a limb for fear of repercussions.

To this day I am grateful to God for sending me help at my moment of need. I heard the sound of a truck engine rumbling from far up the street. Fearing it was a military truck, I rolled over to the edge of the ditch to look like a corpse. From the corner of my eye I saw the truck speeding down the street in my direction. Sure enough, it wasn't one of those jungle green military trucks. I stuck my head up a bit just to confirm, and yes, it was a civilian vehicle.

At that point I didn't care whose it was or wherever it was headed. All I wanted was a one-way ticket out of Mogadishu. I defied my fears, sprang to my feet and headed towards the middle of the road. I signaled the driver to slow down. He decelerated a bit and then he seemed to change his mind and slammed his foot on the gas pedal. I guess he was wondering what on earth I was doing in that part of the city at a time when there was virtually no business to conduct.

Judging by his driving speed as he approached where I was, the driver must have been escaping from danger too. By sheer luck I managed to cling onto the side bars on the truck's body. The driver swung the truck into zigzag motions as if to shed me off, but I held on tight. I then heaved my weight upward and collapsed in a heap on the empty truck's cold metallic floor. My ankle hurt even more as I landed on my left foot, but that was nothing compared to the sense of desperation that had engulfed me a few moments earlier, dodging bullets and running for my dear life. The truck sped out of the city.

In retrospect, I think I now understand the meaning of hammer and anvil as a battlefield strategy. That's what the soldiers had used on us. After defying the four soldiers' request to return home, they had feigned harmlessness and allowed us to pass. They knew we were going to run into a wall of more armed soldiers, and then both teams would hit us proper, trapped there in between. To this day I have never known who else escaped the harrowing death trap, as I have never again seen any of my colleagues, nor heard of their whereabouts.

It was dark when I finally got back home. I found my panicked family waiting for me—desperate to escape the encroaching gunfire, but resolute not to leave without me. They had been waiting for hours though none of them knew for how long I would be gone or whether I would return.

There was no time to waste. We got busy stashing whatever we could into suitcases, bags and sacks. There were more valuables that we could have carried, but this was not one of those well-planned relocations where you call a courier service to arrange the boxes for you in a waiting truck. Rather, it was a question of picking what was necessary for basic survival.

Within minutes, there was a truck hooting at the gate. It was almost full; I wondered how we were going to fit an entire family of fourteen and our luggage. Mom went to negotiate with the driver, and all I could see the driver do was shake his head in disagreement.

Then mom ran back to us and told us there wasn't enough space for the entire luggage, we had to leave some of it in the house, hoping to come back for more when the situation got less tense. After all, we weren't leaving our beautiful house and city life for good. How could we?

We thus heaved over the truck just a few items, mainly Dad and Mom's suitcases, food, two jerry cans of water, and some clothes wrapped in a duvet. Thereafter, we squeezed ourselves aboard the truck—the fourteen of us. There were other families on board too, and lucky for them, they had gotten some space for their luggage.

All this time I hadn't dared to ask where we were going. I had been through too much in just a few hours to care about anything apart from the fact that I was alive.

As the truck sped out of Mogadishu, I thanked God for saving my life. The thought of a bullet hitting me came to my mind each time the vehicle hit a bump. I kept ducking, so terrified, but afraid to tell anyone what had happened in the city center. I was so traumatized that I couldn't speak of the fate of any of the boys with whom I had gone to what should have been peaceful protests.

I would sandwich myself between my sister to the left and my brother to the right each time we came to a roadblock manned by soldiers. I didn't dare look at any one of them—I feared that they might turn their weapons on us, just like the soldiers in the city had done earlier that afternoon.

# Chapter 3
## On the Run to Afgoye

Leaving Mogadishu was one of the most emotional experiences of my young life. I was born and had lived all my life in our peaceful neighborhood of Medina. Unlike other city suburbs that were swarming with people, Medina district was quite spacious with each home set in a fenced compound with beautiful trees, flowers and lawns. I adored the air of relative affluence that characterized our lifestyle. I had become accustomed to accompanying my mom and elder brothers and sisters for shopping in the city's downtown. It had never occurred to me even once that something terrible could happen and cause me and my family to leave all this behind.

Unfortunately we were now on our way out of Mogadishu. Mom told me and my younger sisters, Kowsar and Hani, that we were heading to Afgoye, a city about twenty miles away. Among those travelling with us in the old hired Italian-made Fiat truck was my aunt Mariam, who was pregnant and almost due. Sandwiched between the many pieces of luggage were my three uncles and their families, four of my married sisters, their husbands and kids, as well as a few of my neighbors. There were two of my school teachers and their families escaping with us too. In total we were thirty-two passengers.

No one knew how life would turn out at Afgoye. All I was certain of is that we shared hatred for this cruel disruption to what had been a good and peaceful life.

Mom could see the confusion written all over her children's faces, and I could tell she was worried too. However, she had to show strength even in this state of uncertainty. Like us, she didn't know anything about where we were going to settle once we got to Afgoye, yet she had to remain optimistic if only to give us some hope.

"Whatever transpires at Afgoye," Mom told us, "We will only remain there for a week or so before coming back to Mogadishu. After all, we have left most of our belongings in the house at Medina, and it would be a great loss if we never went back for them."

My brother Abdullahi couldn't agree more. "We've left the city in a hurry and it looks like the fighting in Mogadishu is coming to a climax. It appears that Barre will be defeated, someone else will be able to take over and lead the nation, and we can go home. I see this happening in just a matter of days."

As the truck's engine hummed on and the truck's body swung from side to side on the bumpy road, I suddenly got a vision of what life was—a scary bumpy road to God knows where. The pace of the journey was rather slow, mainly because we used poorly maintained short cuts through the bushes as opposed to the main highway, which had an unreasonable number of roadblocks, some manned by government forces and others by rogue gunmen out to extort travelers. Had there been roadblocks by militia fighters of the opposition, we might not have survived.

Since the war had broken out, erecting roadblocks on major highways had become an easy way for anyone with a gun to earn money. Many people had guns, so they made their money in this cruel way. In many cases, they would shoot and badly wound vehicle occupants or even kill them for a chance to search for any valuables in the vehicles. The goons were taking advantage of the fact that, as people fled the war, they did so with what they considered most precious. As all this transpired, there wasn't a single politician of national stature coming out to urge an end to the conflict. Most of them had already left with their families for safer countries across the world, leaving ordinary citizens to butcher each other

With the prevailing lawlessness, it was not uncommon for the gunmen to drive away with the vehicles they robbed at the roadblocks. The most preferred models were the four wheel drives, which would be used to hunt down those driving through the bushes to avoid falling prey to the madness on the highways. The majority of these off-road monsters would then be converted into "technicals," get mounted with machine guns and taken to the most active war zones.

This was the kind of terror that now ruled the areas around Mogadishu. Fleeing the war whether by day or night had become a complicated and nerve-wracking affair and most people only got to their destinations by God's grace. Silently, all of us kept saying a three-part prayer: "God save us from the government forces who might mistake us for opposition spies. Save us too from

the opposition fighters who might confuse us for government sympathizers or simply target us for any other
reason including clan affiliation. God save us too from
the gunmen without names at the roadblocks and those
hunting down our people with Land Cruisers in the
bushes, as they might confuse us for rich men escaping
with valuable treasures."

Though fearful of what lurked ahead, the trucks kept
moving. For long durations of time we went without ut-
tering a word—just listening to the engine's monotonous rumbling. Everyone seemed lost in his or her own
thoughts. It was a tense journey. For me, the dark night
sky with tiny stars suspended so far away reflected the
answer to my question about the distance between us
and any kind of help. The stars were a mockery of the
proverbial saying about the light at the end of the tunnel.
Here, the tunnel was the night's darkness. The light, on
the other hand, were the stars forming a glittering city
thousands of miles away in the skies. For now, reaching
the city of stars felt like an unachievable dream; I therefore chose to close my eyes and wish time would just fly
away so that my family and I could find ourselves in a
quiet and peaceful place.

Sometimes the overloaded truck would tip to one side
so much that we feared it would topple over. You could
see the fear written all over the faces of the people on the
side of the incline. The wooden boxes with their belongings would squeak or snap under the shifting weight. But
what made me feel most insecure were the big clouds
of dust that the convoy was leaving behind. I shouldn't
have minded about this now that it was night, but the

beams of light that the trucks ahead and those behind us had created with their headlights were guaranteed to attract attention towards the fleeing convoy. Along the dusty roads, we had joined a convoy of about eighteen other trucks overflowing with people and belongings all crammed in together. Such an exodus of overloaded trucks was guaranteed to attract attention from pro-government and opposition fighters or robbers. We feared it was a question of when - not whether we were going to be attacked.

It was such thoughts that made me feel as though traveling in the convoy was by far riskier than remaining in Mogadishu. I reasoned that it was easier for anyone to spot a convoy of overloaded trucks than someone hiding inside a house as big as the one we had left behind. Did the grown-ups know more than I did? Probably! But the journey had started and there seemed to be no turning back. I went back to reciting my silent three-part prayer.

## A Taste of Life in Afgoye

It was half past eight in the evening when we got to Afgoye. Dad would have preferred it if the truck had been able to take us to the stadium or a school's compound, but the traffic jam on the city's roads made this impossible. The driver thus parked at what appeared to be the most convenient place—by the roadside.

Though we hadn't experienced any terrible incidents along the way, the emotional drain of the journey made us feel like we had traveled to Kathmandu and back on foot. However, I was perhaps the most excited of all people to hear Dad's voice asking us to alight.

I hurriedly crawled out from under the wooden luggage where I had been hiding for most of the journey, climbed over the truck's cabin, slid down the side, and then jumped off to the dusty ground. I could feel the heat radiating from the truck's dusty rear wheels, and I could tell the vehicle had been tested to its limits by the poor roads.

There was no electricity in the area of the city where we found ourselves, so the place was in darkness except for the vehicles' headlights and the tiny lights shining from the thousands of tents that lined the city's streets and alleys. With no idea of what to do or where to go next, my family and I just stood there by the truck's side, waiting for everyone else to step down.

So, we thought, we were the only ones who knew of the peace in Afgoye? To say the city was overcrowded would be an understatement. Everywhere there were people who, just like us, had escaped the fighting and had sought refuge in this city. The streets were full of strangers, going to and coming from God knows where. Interestingly, though some walked in groups, there were hardly any conversations amongst them. Much of the city was disturbingly quiet.

As my brothers, sisters and neighbors got off the truck, I couldn't help but notice the surprised look on their faces upon seeing where we had ended up. It was clear that unlike the double beds and duvets we had left in our Mogadishu home, there weren't going to be comfortable places for all of us to rest till morning. Still, no one could picture themselves sleeping under the luggage in the truck.

As we stood there, two more trucks drove up to where we were standing and emptied their human cargo right there beside us. I couldn't tell how many people each truck carried, but there must have been close to a hundred each, since we immediately sensed the overcrowding. Long before all the people could get off, three more trucks parked a few feet from the first two, and soon we were lost in the multitude. In a little while, there were trucks squeezing into any available space and spewing out more people into the already badly congested space. With each truck, the sense of helplessness, confusion and vulnerability increased in scale.

Food was foremost on the minds of most of my siblings. We were ravenous, especially children like me who hadn't eaten anything since morning. The night was cold and I wouldn't have minded a jacket, though unfortunately I hadn't carried one. I just stood there beside the truck, in my blue T-shirt, brown trousers, and old black leather shoes. From some distance you could hear my teeth clattering in the dark and cold night.

After exchanging few thoughts about the next course of action, my brothers Wali, Abdirizak and I decided to look around for a shop so that we could buy some bread and drinks. We set out towards what looked like a shop a few meters down the road. From a distance we could see some human movement in a manner that suggested some commercial activity. We made haste, running through the large mass of people.

We squeezed through the thick crowds. But on getting there, we found it was a scramble for sleeping tents that were being issued from the back of a pickup truck. It wasn't a shop after all. Upon further enquiry, we were reliably informed that businesses were already closed and there wasn't a place to buy bread for a hungry soul. Word had it that all supplies in shops had already been exhausted.

We walked back to the truck feeling deflated. But we had at least gotten an idea that there were tents being issued for which we could hopefully scramble. The news seemed to brighten everyone. Therefore, we were asked to remain on standby, just in case we got wind of more supplies.

Soon after, a small pickup truck similar to the one we had seen with tents drove past our truck. Wali was quick to identify it, and motioned dad and two of my brothers-in-law to follow him into the darkness. No one else seemed to know what was going on.

The pickup stopped a few meters down the road. There was a heavily built man on its back, who made an announcement for people to queue for tents. But before he had even finished those words, he had already been shoved down the truck as a sea of people fell over themselves scrambling for the supplies.

My brother Abdirizak and I ran towards the truck too, just in case there was something we could do to help my dad and the others. In the light of the emerging moon we saw it all.

Yes, there was Dad, the strongest pillar in my life, pushing, shoving, falling over and getting back on his feet, sweat all over his brow, scrambling for humanitarian assistance! There was dust all over his shoulders, on the back of his jacket and on his hair.

Beside him were Wali and two of my brother-in-laws, all showing a kind of aggressiveness and menace I had never seen before! I couldn't believe that this was the kind of life to which my mentors and role models had been reduced. I really hated war! In a mixture of anger and humiliation, I wept as I hurried back towards the truck that had now become home. I just couldn't stand the sight of Dad wrestling with hustlers over something he would under normal circumstances have ordered to be delivered to our doorstep.

It was around 10:30 p.m. when dad and my brothers returned. They had been able to get just three white tents, certainly not enough for us all. The next hassle was finding a place to set up the tents. It is hard to imagine just how precious a few inches of earth had suddenly become.

There was literally no place left to set up a simple tent, because of the hundreds of people and hundreds of trucks that had packed in the little space by the road within hours. We thus ended up erecting the tents on the fringes of the dusty road connecting Afgoye and Mogadishu. Actually, we just set up where our truck had parked, squeezed ourselves into the various tents and prayed for a safe daybreak.

I didn't sleep a wink because of the constant movement of people around the tent. Four people, including the truck's driver, squeezed into the little polythene-lined sack tents and this meant that not all our body parts could fit under the shelter. So, my feet remained out in the cold, no matter how much I tried to squeeze them in. I nonetheless wouldn't dare mention this to anyone. I felt I shouldn't be a bother because my feet would be safe as long as they were under the truck and the truck's driver was in our tent.

Occasionally there were sounds of trucks driving down the road a few meters from where we slept, and the resulting dust would suddenly force us all into a coughing and sneezing competition. Worse, I feared that a vehicle could veer off the road and ram into us.

Though mom had promised that Afgoye was only going to be a temporary place of refuge while we monitored the situation in Mogadishu, I wondered how many more cold and miserable nights we were going to endure before Mogadishu had stabilized and we would be on our way back home.

## Elusive Hope

Days came and went as we were all glued to our radios hoping for some good news. Everyone followed the proceedings keenly, though most of the time there wasn't sufficient information to help one make important decisions. Instead people were left to analyze the unpredictable situation, much like a pilot flying in bad weather with faulty instruments.

Lack of information was a major cause of anxiety: no one knew how far violence actually was from Afgoye, the city of internal refugees. And the more we lacked answers to important questions, the more people filled the information gaps with conspiracy theories and made worst-case scenarios seem like immediate possibilities.

In the meantime, opposition forces kept advancing in their mission to conquer key neighborhoods around Mogadishu. Government forces weren't giving up either, so they came out with their guns blazing to meet the opposition fighters. Gradually, Afgoye started falling within view of the fights, and suddenly it was right in the middle of their crosshairs.

To both the opposition and government forces, Afgoye was a strategic city, as it served as an important gateway to Mogadishu and to other major cities in southern Somalia. That meant that whoever controlled the city could easily block the opponent's key supplies, which would eventually lead to defeat.

Compared to neighboring cities, Afgoye was comparatively more developed, thanks to the modest investments it had attracted from Gulf States in the 1980s. Much of the investments had consequently trickled down to earn the city some good roads, decent shopping outlets, as well as reliable water, sanitation and electricity. The Emir of Kuwait used to visit the town during the holy month of Ramadan, raising the city's religious status.

After a week's stay at Afgoye, news came through that the government was losing control of Mogadishu. This was a difficult situation to interpret as no one had any idea of how the new state was going to operate, or even whether the government was going to make a comeback. The entire country remained tense, only hoping that whatever transpired, peace got restored so that everyone could go back to their normal lives.

There was, however, news of more government troops heading into Mogadishu to hedge the failing government, and yet still more rebel fighters surrounding the city, something that made matters appear suspended in the balance, heightening the sense of uncertainty in the air.

As a boy, I kept wondering why all this was happening, and why the leadership couldn't see a problem of such magnitude coming and find ways to avert it. Why couldn't the government and the opposition agree on something so we could go back to school?

Nevertheless, the more I thought of school, the more I feared the uncertainty of returning to an empty class. I feared more the thought of discovering who else might have died in the armed conflict that had become the order of the day in Mogadishu. But still I yearned for the friendships that I had left behind.

## Escape to Kismayu

As the days went by, we kept listening for good news, but things kept getting gloomier. The intensity of war in Mogadishu made any thoughts of return sound crazy. Presently, the news in the air was that the opposition and more government forces were in contest over Afgoye, each side determined to get the upper hand.

Earlier on, this had sounded like just one of the rumors being spread by conspiracy theorists. But positioning of land cruisers fitted with large machine guns and missile launchers on top, "technicals," along the road from Afgoye to Mogadishu only served to confirm everyone's worst fears. It was clear that unless something drastic happened, it was just a matter of days before the air we breathed in the city became choked with thunderous sounds, smoke, dust, and helpless wails.

Given what we had been through in Mogadishu, thanks to procrastination, Dad was not going to have his family entangled in such a mishap again. We weren't going to wait until another missile hit the neighborhood to force us into motion.

Dad summoned us all around the truck in which we had travelled in to Afgoye. Somehow the driver had remained with us, and had become part of us. It is amazing just how disaster, scarcity and feelings of vulnerability can cause people to stick together as we had done. Dad announced that we were to escape from Afgoye before the worst befell the city. We were to gather our every belonging -- including tents and relief supplies -- and board the truck for the journey to the port city of Kismayu along the Indian Ocean, about 280 miles to the south.

It was by now clear that peace wasn't going to visit Mogadishu anytime soon. What had initially been thought as a simple battle to oust Siad Barre now had all the signs of a long drawn out atrocious war whose end no one could predict. With the dream of returning to Mogadishu becoming ever more elusive, the idea was to escape to Kismayu via Shalanbood so that we could easily flee into the neighboring state of Kenya via the Indian Ocean if need be.

On a bright Thursday morning we packed all we owned into the truck. As we heaved the suitcases onboard the truck, I overheard Mom asking Dad whether his headache and back pains had subsided. "Could Dad have been badly injured during the scramble for sleeping tents the week before?" I wondered.

Two of my former teachers and three former neighbors pleaded on behalf of their families to go with us, though they didn't have any more cash left on them to pay for transport. The truck was once again going to be full capacity just as it were when we came to Afgoye. Dad accepted, although he too didn't know where he was going to get the resources to feed so many hungry mouths on this long and uncertain journey. Similarly, like the journey to Afgoye, there wasn't a definite place where we were going to set up base—it was just an escape founded on hope for a better place for refuge compared to Afgoye and Mogadishu.

At around noon, the truck driver started the engine. We hurriedly boarded it and bid Afgoye goodbye. We were to have a brief stopover at Shalanbood, about forty-three miles away, before heading further south if the security situation allowed.

Just like the journey to Afgoye, we weren't going to use the main road for obvious security reasons. We were not ready to have our luggage searched at gun point, so we headed for the bush route once again. The truck followed tracks left on the grasslands by other vehicles leaving Afgoye for Shalanbood. Luckily, the driver was an old hand in these routes. As I was later to learn, he had spent close to twelve of his fifteen years of experience as a driver ferrying charcoal from the interior to the port city of Kismayu.

We had been journeying for about thirty minutes when word came that Afgoye had been engulfed in full fighting.

In the ensuing mêlée, dozens of civilians had been killed, thereby triggering civilians to flee again. We couldn't thank Dad enough for the timely decision he had made to take us to safety. We thanked the Lord that the tensions in Afgoye were now behind us, as we couldn't imagine what would have happened to us had we been caught up in the conflict.

We then drove on through the expansive grassland that was part of the route that we had taken. About half-an-hour after the Afgoye update, there came some more breaking news that there have been clashes reported between various armed groups about twenty miles from Shalanbood on the way from Afgoye. The heavy exchange of fire is ongoing, though no statistics have been issued regarding the number of casualties.

This made us freeze. We were about thirteen miles from Shalanbood and not too far away from the main road. The truck immediately changed course and headed towards some nearby high bushes. We couldn't proceed towards Shalanbood; instead we had to take cover as we examined the situation.

Dad came over to the back of the truck, if only to reassure us that all would be well. That was very brave of him since we had already started hearing sounds of gunfire. Although he was making an effort to give us hope, for the first time in my life I saw him getting scared. The sound of gunfire kept getting louder by the moment. We soon heard movements and gunfire coming from the very bush in which our truck was hidden. It was nerve wracking, since no one knew what would happen next or when the firing would stop.

We tried to hide deeper beneath the luggage in the truck, but there were too many of us to cover. To say that we were frightened to death is an understatement. We fervently prayed that God might see us through this hell-on-earth experience. In the midst of this, Aunt

Mariam went into labor. Her big day had come and little Kamal, the name proposed for the unborn infant, was rearing to get out of the womb not knowing that he was coming into a world from which even adults were struggling to exist.

Mariam gave a desperate groan and I heard someone curse under his breath. I guess Mariam had been withholding the pain for far too long and it was only when she cried out the second time that we knew things were desperate.

Mom called to Mariam: "You mean it's time?"

"Yes, my sister. I feel like I might die with the baby inside me," Mariam replied.

"If you die, my sister, I would have no reason to live too. We are here for you and we will take care of your to the best of our ability," mom said. There was a strange note of courage in her voice. She crawled out from her hideout under the luggage. There were sounds of gunfire, but mom made her way through the mess of luggage onboard the truck to where Mariam was hiding.

"If there are men in this truck, I mean real men, let them come and help me take Mariam out to the bush," came mom's challenging voice.

No one moved. Aunt's cries were getting louder and more frequent, but the thought of getting away from the truck's safety was simply absurd.

"Come on! Are those not men fighting out there? Are they not risking their lives for something they believe in? If you believe in life, this is the time to prove it!"

Wali was the first to move. He crawled out of the luggage. He then did the unthinkable. He threw open the truck's rear cover. "If mom is risking her life for Aunt Mariam, then we must all do the same. Everyone get out of this fake sense of security, we can't watch one of us die while we can help!"

I was scared like hell, but I too crawled out and made an attempt to help. Mom motioned me to move away indicating that it was none of my business. I gave way and two of my sisters moved in. Mom had already wrapped a kanga (African garment) around Mariam's waist. She was visibly in pain and she kept mumbling things I couldn't comprehend. The three of them heaved Mariam off the truck and placed her on a patch of grass under some overgrown bushes a few meters from the truck.

The sound of gunfire had moved to a distance, but the metallic crack of the guns still sounded lethal. Peeking over the truck's top rails, you could occasionally see troops make their maneuvers and drive away across the field, then more intense gunfire.

After about forty minutes, Aunt Mariam was escorted back to the truck. My sister Fardowsa was carrying a newborn and she told us his name was Kamal. He was a beloved child born in a battlefield away from any known hospital or health center.

Realizing that there were grave risks involved whatever decision we made—whether remaining in the bush, returning to Afgoye or proceeding to Shalanbood—my brother Wali and Dad decided that proceeding to Shalanbood and later to Kismayu was the option of lesser evil. So we headed to Shalanbood. We stayed there for four days, mainly to help Aunt Mariam recover and have Kamal's health checked by a medic, before proceeding to

Kismayu. We were informed by the locals that the police could provide an escort car for us if we could pay for the service. After Dad had made the payments at the local police office, he was asked to wait for a few more trucks on their way over there so we could proceed together to Kismayu under police escort.

It was on a Monday afternoon when we once again boarded the truck and joined a convoy of fifteen trucks en route to Kismayu. There were two police vehicles, one ahead and the other at the tail end of the convoy. From the reports we had gathered, it seemed like we had left the worst behind us.

So the truck rolled on to safety. Unlike the journey to Afgoye and later to Shalanbood, which had roadblocks and the perpetual risk of running into a battlefield, the regions beyond Shalanbood were calm and we now seemed to have found the semblance of peace that we had yearned for over the past month. The road to Kismayu was a smooth ride. There was an air of freedom, a sense of calmness that seemed to soothe our nerves. I was beginning to feel good about life once again, and I wished someone could lead us in a chorus as the truck rolled on towards freedom.

However, this feeling was suddenly shattered forty-five minutes into the journey by a loud bang and a series of gunshots. I saw someone fall off the truck's top rails and get trapped in the luggage. There was another splash of blood onto the truck's inner wall and before we realized it we were all drenched in blood. Another person gave a desperate scream before collapsing head first over my Mom, then rolling over to where Aunt Mariam was recuperating with baby Kamal. The truck sped off amidst our screaming and then abruptly came to a stop where the driver thought it was safe to park. There were more sounds of gunshots that lasted for about ten minutes, and we could tell they were at a close range from where we were.

It was a horrifying experience, and no one dared to move. We remained tucked under the luggage as we had gotten accustomed to whenever things got this crazy. Without even taking time to check out the fate of the wounded among us, the truck once again sped off down the road and caught up with the rest of the convoy.

Our convoy of sixteen trucks finally made a stopover at Barawe, a town sixteen miles from Shalanbood, to take stock of the casualties. There were fourteen people injured from all the trucks, and they were taken to a small health facility at Barawe for treatment. The convoy had also suffered eight fatalities, all of whom were buried in the same town. Among those who had died in our truck was Abdimalik, who had been a teacher in Mogadishu, and two middle-aged men who had travelled with us from Mogadishu to Afgoye and were now travelling with us to Kismayu.

Unlike the passengers in our truck, who had come from the same neighborhood in Mogadishu, most of the other trucks had picked up passengers from Afgoye, who were largely strangers to each other. None of the drivers seemed certain about the number of passengers on board any of the trucks, so it was difficult figuring out how many of the passengers might have fallen off the speeding trucks and died.

We also learned that the two police escort cars that had accompanied us from Shalanbood had been hit with mortar, though no one knew of the fate of the police officers travelling in the vehicles. No one seemed certain about the motive of the attack.

While still at Barawe, we received sad news of the death of my beloved uncle, Abdullahi Ali Farasle and his son, Mohamed Abdullahi Ali. My uncle was a well-respected man and a peace activist. He had played a significant role in peace negotiations between the government and various opposition factions. When the civil war started, my uncle, who was a member of the national reconciliation committee, had shuttled between Nairobi and Mogadishu with the hope of finding a peaceful resolution to the war. He had returned from Nairobi in the last week of December 1990. According to Dad, this time round Abdullahi seemed convinced that there wasn't going to be a peaceful resolution to the conflict in Somalia any time soon.

He had moved his family from Mogadishu to Qoryeeley, a distance of sixty-three miles. At the time, Qoryeeley seemed calm. During our brief stopover at Shalanbood, Dad had spoken with uncle Abdullahi by phone and convinced him that it was wiser to plan a complete exit from Somalia, and that Kismayu presented a good route to Kenya. Uncle Abdullahi was thus supposed to link up with us at Kismayu as we surveyed the situation from there.

It was on his way to Shalanbood en route to Kismayu that fighters from one of the opposition groups stopped uncle Abdullahi's vehicle and ordered everyone to come out. The fighters then gunned him down before descending on the family members, killing them one by one at point blank range. They only spared a few shaken children, including two of my uncle's grandsons, Gurey and Mohamed. Gurey and Mohamed would spend weeks in Shalanbood before they too left for Kismayu with an auntie who had earlier fled from Qoryeeley and safely made it to Shalanbood. At the time, I could not understand why he was targeted. I later learned that all of the violence was not random and that some people were targeted including my uncle because of the clan they belonged to.

After our tragic incident and brief stopover at Barawe, we continued our trip to Kismayu. At that time Barawe seemed relatively calm though there were signs of trouble coming as we kept hearing of advances by various armed forces. Not willing to stay longer to prove the stories right or wrong, we took the road towards the town of Jilib, seventy-two miles from Barawe. We stopped over in the town for two days before proceeding to Kasumo and finally to Kismayu.

During our stay in Kismayu, the situation was always tense, but far better than anywhere else that we had been since leaving Mogadishu. Here at least we lived in good homes and in relative safety. People in the city were friendly and they didn't look as terrified by the war as those of us who had come from Mogadishu.

Although I was born in Mogadishu, Kismayu is the area from which my family mostly hails. My family is among those Somali families that were most affected by colonization. With the coming of the foreign powers, not just Somalis as a whole, or my clan, but even my family had been divided into three parts and forced to move apart. As a result, I have family members who are today part of Ethiopia, Kenya and Somalia—each having different national identities. Therefore coming to Kismayu felt like coming back home. I had hope of attending school once again and I was lucky to make a few friends, though we never grew as close as the friends I had grown up with in Mogadishu.

When the news reached Kismayu that the Somali President Mohamed Siyad Barre had fled from Mogadishu, tension gripped Kismayu and no one knew what to expect. This was mainly because the city had been under government forces, and Barre's defeat would easily motivate opposition fighters to push for the takeover of Kismayu.

Kismayu was and still remains one of Somalia's most important seaports. From history I have learned that much of the city's prosperity came from export of livestock and charcoal to the Middle East. The city also served as an important entry point for merchandise, in addition to the city's industries, which included meat and fish processing, leather tanning and sugar refining.

Fishing was an important occupation for the city's residents and there were vessels of all sizes docking at the port to offload their cargo to waiting trucks to take the stocks to the processing facilities. However, perhaps the greatest value attached to the city was the potential of substantial oil deposits around the area. It was rumored that the city and its surrounding areas were sitting on a vast oil field and that explorations were going to commence in due course. This was going to usher in a new era of prosperity not only for the city of Kismayu and its residents, but for all of Somalia and Eastern Africa.

With the fall of Barre's government in June 1991, factional forces began their push to take over the control of the city from the pro-government forces. It was at that point that all hell broke loose. Contrary to our earlier thoughts that we could escape the war through the Indian Ocean into Kenya, there wasn't a dream further removed from reality than that.

As the fighters crashed in Kismayu, the matrix of the conflict changed faster than anyone could have imagined. The ultimate prize for all parties, including the opposition and government forces, became capturing the city's lifeline: the port. Whichever side won the port could levy taxes and get sustenance for its military activities, and possibly set up an independent administration for the city. The various units also wanted to capitalize on the port city's strategic advantage of being a key gateway to the outside world, as well as its close proximity to Kenya.

This meant that whoever conquered the city had access to a key trade gateway and would effectively block out the rival's access to material and financial supplies from the outside world. For this strategic reason, no one was willing to give in, effectively converting the port and anywhere else close to the ocean into a battlefield.

There was heavy exchange of fire in the city streets on almost a daily basis and escaping through the sea was now out of question. Because we had learned from our previous experience, we weren't going to hang around and hope that the situation would calm down and return to normalcy. We followed our instinct and fled the city. We were on the run again.

My brother Wali had taken charge of leadership now that Dad was ailing. The constant headaches he had suffered since leaving Mogadishu had been diagnosed as arising from high blood pressure, so we did the best we could to keep him from worrying much. Wali decided that we were not going to gamble with life in Somalia anymore. It was time to find a more plausible solution, and that meant finding our way to Kenya.

# Chapter 4
## Gateway to Kenya

Much as we dreaded what we had already gone through in our escape from Mogadishu, there didn't seem an easy way out of Somalia. Now that escape via the port city of Kismayu was out of the question, we had to cut our way right through Somalia's burning cities and pray for the best. Once again we boarded the truck for the long treacherous journey through Afmadow, Qooqaani, Dhoobley and eventually to Liboi, which served as an official refugees' gateway into Kenya.

When we crossed the border into Kenya, it felt like a big achievement. We had successfully navigated our way through Somalia's war zones. We had withstood the hunger and thirst. We had overcome the many obstacles that stood between us and the objects of our hope. At last we felt free. My sisters hugged each other and cried, unable to withstand the emotional strain any longer.

I felt as if a large burden that I had been carrying for ages had been heaved off my family's shoulders. The mental anguish my family and I had suffered during the previous two months since the war had broken out had turned us into short-tempered people, the kind that viewed everything with skepticism and mistrust. But this time I trusted that crossing over to Kenya would give us a second chance at life.

With Somalia and its never-ending conflicts behind us, we could walk without having to look over our shoulders in fear of what lurked behind us for the first time. I could tell that Dad too felt at ease, though he seemed a bit anxious about what life as refugees had in store for his once-prosperous family, now reduced to asylum seekers.

We went through the usual security checks at the Liboi border post. There were long queues of refugees waiting for clearance and registration. We had anticipated this, owing to the reports we had heard from others who had crossed the border before and then returned to Somalia for one reason or another. Consequently, we knew that we would be queuing under the scorching tropical sun for a long time.

The Liboi border post was a small immigration facility set up in a remote and inhospitable area in what was previously Kenya's North Frontier District (NFD). The compound consisted of three short trees and an old wooden office block. Behind the block were a few makeshift houses made of iron sheets that housed the security officers on duty at the post. At least that was the part visible to me from the queue.

Around the camp were armed Administration Police (AP) and members of the Kenyan military. While some conducted searches of the refugees to ensure none were armed or attempting to smuggle weapons into Kenya, others stood by on guard or leaned against the walls of the nearby structures, with guns strapped over their shoulders. The inspection for arms was necessary, as one soldier explained to Dad, who, though complying, jokingly enquired about the exercise.

"You see, there are good Somalis and as you have already seen by now, there are some who aren't nice at all," explained one tall dark soldier, as he ran his hands along Dad's flanks, as if hoping to feel a gun tucked away.

"I understand that," replied Dad. "But do you still expect the not so nice ones to cross the border through the legally designated routes?"

"Yes and no," replied the soldier, now moving on to search my brother Abdirizak.

"You see, you can't get to the refugee camps without security clearance. There might be bad elements wishing to register as refugees and then use weapons to carry out criminal activities here. We have to prevent that. However, we aren't oblivious to the porous nature of our borders, which means criminals can cross into Kenya at any point along the several hundreds of miles of open fields that we call our borders," explained the soldier, moving on down the queue. That left me wondering what the purpose of the body search was if anyone could cross over at any point. Was it just another small humiliation?

About six hours had passed since we got to Liboi. It was a quarter to four in the afternoon when we were allowed into the presence of the officers from the United Nation's High Commission for Refugees (UNHCR). I woke up Mom and Fardowsa, who had succumbed to sleep in the shade while we held their place in the queue.

As dad and I stepped into one of the makeshift offices, the four officers on duty were busy entering the data of the refugees they had already collected, into large books. From the look on the face of the female officer before whose old wooden desk we were standing, I could see this was a monotonous exercise. They gathered information about the number of refugees streaming in on a daily basis in order to aid in the planning for humanitarian assistance.

When our time came, the officer looked up. "Mohamed?" she asked. No one answered. "Almost every male Somali is called Mohamed or Abdi. Are you an exception?" Dad smiled. I found myself smiling too, aware that our brother Abdirizak was waiting outside.

"Ok, pardon me. You may give me your story now, beginning with your names and the part of Somalia you come from," said the lady at the desk.

It was Dad who gave all the responses and any other information that was required regarding our family. The woman did most of the listening, and then entered a few details into the record book. A young male officer went out to verify whether the information that Dad had given was correct. As the door was ajar, I could see the officer count the members of our family present for registration. He then proceeded to call them out by name. Satisfied, he came back.

There wasn't much time to delve into more personal issues, so we were each given a piece of paper with a unique number and asked to retain it for as long as we were to stay in Kenya.

These were the numbers we were supposed to use when collecting food rations. Later we used them to apply for our alien identity cards.

Ironically, this whole process excited me. I was no longer Hamse, but a new statistical figure on a small white piece of paper. If I lost the paper, I would be lost from the global radar. The same case applied to Dad, Mom, my brothers, and my sisters and their husbands. We were mere numbers and statistics. Nobody bothered to find out what our real identities were, or if we had any dreams or ambitions beyond attaining refugee status.

We were shown the route to follow towards Dadaab, now the world's largest refugee camp hosting in excess of 630,000 refugees. Thus, off to Dadaab we went. From afar we could see acres upon acres of desert land covered in white tents.

As we drew closer to the camp, we started meeting people going about their business. I could tell they were mostly Somalis by their slim physique and the head-scarves of women.

I will never forget this dark woman with a yellow head scarf carrying a scantily dressed child on her back. On her head this woman carried a large wobbly pile of firewood tied together with a thin piece of rope. She supported the firewood with her left hand, while the right one supported the child on her back. She appeared disturbed, as she walked along muttering things to herself. She looked quite mean and did not seem pleased to see us come to the camp.

I wondered why she would be so agitated at seeing people successfully escape Somali's armed conflict. I hated to imagine that this would be how malnourished and unhappy my sisters and Mom would look after having stayed in the camp for a while. My heart sank at the thought.

## Discovering Life in Dadaab

There was a team of officials from CARE, UNHCR and representatives of other organizations ready to meet us on our arrival at the camp. They ushered us into the UN-HCR office near the camp's entrance to confirm that we were in the camp legally. We were then given a basic orientation, which mainly focused on how life in a refugee camp might differ from the kind of life we had previously lived in Somalia.

Dad, Mom and Wali were taken around to the various offices from which we could seek assistance in case of medical emergencies and for dispute resolution. This was done while the rest of us waited outside the UNHCR offices. In the meantime, more refugees trickled in to be served and shown around.

Later, we were led to a group of refugees and were introduced to each other as members of the soon to be formed new neighborhood group inside the camp. This was one of the strategies the camp administration was using to ensure easy adaptation to the new kind of life in the camp. It was also a way of fostering social integration among the refugees and creating a sense of belonging. It was at this point that the camp's rules were read to us. We were informed of our limited freedom, which was a far cry from what local citizens enjoyed.

Refugees were not allowed to engage in trade; even the sale of relief supplies was illegal. If one engaged in physical scuffles or violence, one would rot in a Kenyan prison, notorious for inhumane treatment of prisoners and deaths due to diseases resulting from conditions such as cholera.

From here, we were taken to the site where we would set up our tents to begin life as refugees. We walked for about fifteen minutes along the fringes of the main camp. The camp consisted of hundreds of thousands of white tents with the blue UNHCR logo inscribed on their sides. It was hard to believe that this was our new home until peace returned to Somalia.

From far behind us, we saw a trail of dust as a vehicle sped towards us. We walked on. After about five minutes, the vehicle overtook us and stopped a few meters ahead of us. It was a white UNHCR Toyota Land Cruiser.

Two young men alighted and opened the vehicle's rear carriage section, pulled out ten white tents and called out the names of each family head for the neighborhood group to which we had earlier been assigned. Each head was issued a tent or two, depending on the size of his family. A few more tents were pulled out of the vehicle and issued in the order of the roll call. Dad's name wasn't called; there were clearly no more tents left in the vehicle.

I saw the UNHCR and CARE officials retreat to some space beside the Land Cruiser. The more they discussed, the more they appeared to disagree. We could tell that something was amiss though we didn't want to speculate. In the meantime, the families that had been issued tents proceeded to set them up on spaces shown to them by a female UNHCR official who preferred conversing in Swahili rather than English. She looked quite motherly and we hoped that she would come to address us.

She walked farther down, assisting the families in setting up their shelters. As more tents sprang up, she gradually disappeared behind the structures and then the Land Cruiser abruptly drove off, stopping only momentarily on the dusty path to pick up the woman and then proceed down the road. There wasn't any explanation given to us on what to do or what to expect.

Unsure of what would happen next, we set out to assist those already setting up their tents and, in the process, begged them to take us in for the night in case there was further delay in the delivery of our tents. Moments later, and to our excitement, another UNHCR Land Cruiser pulled over just where Mom and my sisters had been waiting.

An officer alighted and issued five tents to mom. These were enough for our family. Thank God, we didn't have to separate and sleep in different "homes" until the following day.

If I thought Afgoye was congested, then Daadab gave the word "congestion" a whole new meaning. There were people everywhere going to God knows where and coming from God knows where. It was like a big slum with absolutely no economic activity and with nothing to keep people busy.

In Dadaab there was no notion of privacy, be it during the day or at night. This was because the harsh desert winds would sometimes blow away an inadequately fastened tent, exposing your precious life's possessions to the whole world.

Due to the vagaries of refugee life, people in Dadaab were irritable and you could tell this by their faces, especially by the premature wrinkles on their foreheads. You would not be mistaken to imagine that people were served vinegar for breakfast each morning.

I abhorred the kind of resignation with which most people carried themselves, and the sense of urgency with which most of them looked for a quarrel, if only to prove to themselves that they still had some essence of life left in them. The slightest provocation could easily earn you the kind of insult that would keep you fuming the whole day. I felt that people needed to engage in something constructive, whatever that would be, to while away the time rather than walk around looking to pick quarrels with others.

Something that I found fun was helping new refugees set up their tents upon arrival. I would show the new boys around the camp, to make them feel welcome. I never asked for anything in return, and for this reason, I would at times be asked by a camp administrator to help elderly or sickly refugees carry water in five gallon jerry cans to their tents.

Perhaps the worst part of life in the refugee camp was trying to obtain water. There were only a handful of taps in the camp. The camp had been set up by the UNHCR as a temporary measure to cater to those fleeing the war in Somalia, in the expectation that the situation would be brought under control and people would be able to return home. But that was not to be. As the fighting in Somalia escalated, so did the influx of refugees into Kenya. Meanwhile, the Kenyan government had designated Dadaab as the only place where refugees from Somalia could be hosted, at least initially.

With time, the crossover rate of around 15,000 people per month exceeded the rate at which resources could be mobilized to cater for the refugees, hence the mess we found ourselves living in. As a result, you could queue at the tap for hours just to fetch a five-gallon jerry can of water, which was hardly sufficient for the entire family.

Access to food was another nightmare. Though there were regular supplies coming in, you still had to queue for prolonged periods at the food stations for your turn to be served.

It was also not uncommon to queue, only to realize at the serving point that you'd forgotten your card in the tent and thus had to run back and fetch it. Upon returning, none of the people would recognize you, let alone accept the fact that you had earlier queued up to the serving point. You therefore had to start the entire process over again.

It was thus normal for one to spend half the day under the scorching sun waiting for the rations of corn, beans, rice and cooking fat. These being weekly or bi-weekly supplies, it meant that almost everyone exhausted their rations at the same time, meaning we would once again be queuing for fresh stock.

Given the tedium of this life, some people had devised ways of surviving. At times you could pay someone to do the queuing on your behalf. The person would call you once he or she got to the service point, so you could collect your ration and pay him on your way home.

Another survival tactic was someone going for fresh stocks even before having exhausted previous supplies. These fresh stocks would then be sold to those who didn't want to go queuing all day for food.

There were people who had somehow managed double and even triple registrations, earning them as many opportunities for collecting supplies. These would then be smuggled out of the camp.

While this trade started as a joke, it later grew into a scandal that warranted wide-scale investigations. It was said that some enterprising refugees would buy surplus food and other supplies around the camp. Of course this was at costs far below prevailing market rates. The entrepreneurs would then collude with security personnel manning the camp to allow trucks to come in and collect the surplus for sale in nearby markets, including Garissa, which served as the capital of Kenya's North Eastern Province.

The quest for money to buy other items not available in the camp had quickly given rise to a number of vices, among them prostitution and muggings. There were many cases of more violent crimes too, including rape and armed robberies. These acts were carried out by organized gangs taking advantage of the inadequate security personnel present in the camp.

Violent crime usually targeted people with connections to Kenyan traders, who were believed to have access to cash through illegal trade. Another target group comprised families that had some of their members living in the diaspora, who would occasionally send cash to the families in the camp for basic sustenance.

Life in Dadaab was horrendous, with occasional outbreaks of cholera. The most affected were usually children.

I know of two small boys who succumbed to the disease. There were stories of children dying in the tents because their parents were sick as well and did not inform anyone that their children were infected. This was the kind of detachment with which people in the camp lived.

Occasionally the camp officials went round checking on the status of the refugees. They advised those with children of school age to enroll them at the makeshift school provided in the camp. They also gave special attention to people with difficulties to enable them to cope with the new kind of life in the refugee camp.

I will never know for sure whether my family fell in this category or whether it was part of a policy to make the camp less congested, but, compared to neighboring families, we seemed to have more frequent visits by the camp's social workers. Two months after settling into Dadaab, we were relocated to Utange Refugee Camp at the Kenyan coast, about 250 miles from Dadaab.

This somehow brought us hope of improved living conditions. As the old adage goes, a change is as good as a rest. We were more than willing to do anything to get out of Dadaab, provided that this would not mean returning to Mogadishu. So, in a convoy of about ten trucks, we headed to Utange in Mombasa.

## Welcome to Utange

It is in Utange that I somehow started accepting the fact that my family and I didn't have much choice as refugees and did not matter much to the world. We had hoped for conditions better than Dadaab, but what we found in Utange made us wish we were back in Kismayu, in spite of the fighting. Congestion was worse than at Dadaab, so much so that we couldn't even get space to settle inside the camp itself. There weren't any tents either, so we had to take care of ourselves by cutting tree branches, tying them up with ropes and strings and filling up the sides with wild grass to make a shelter. This somehow reminded me of Afgoye, where we had had to sleep by the roadside for lack of space within the city.

My brother Wali had great social and networking skills that earned him menial jobs from time to time; with the savings he bought timber and sheets of corrugated iron. Thus we built a better shelter for the family. At Utange, unlike Dadaab, there weren't many social or health facilities. Unlike in Dadaab where people died owing to cholera outbreaks, in Utange the death was caused by malaria. This was because there were fewer aid workers at the camp to take care of the health needs of all the people.

Nonetheless, camp officials did their best to provide mosquito nets and food. The main food provisions were corn, beans, rice and cooking oil. Supplies came either weekly or bi-weekly and they were often enough for basic survival. But, unlike in Dadaab, where you had to walk for long distances in search of firewood, there was plenty of vegetation in Utange, so we got firewood with ease. However, you could clearly tell that it would be just a matter of time before the vegetation would have been cleared due to the rising demand for wood fuel in the area. Eventually, this became a major bone of contention between the refugees and local communities, who felt that we were putting undue pressure on a resource they had struggled to preserve for ages.

Living as refugees meant that we didn't have the luxury of electricity or refrigerators with which to preserve food. Kenya's coast was a generally warm and humid area, this meant that once cooked, food had to be consumed immediately--otherwise it would go bad. The only kind of food that you could preserve was cereals. Vegetables such as tomatoes, cabbage and kale would lose moisture in a matter of days and soon go bad.

Just like at Dadaab, access to water was a challenge. There were always long queues at water points and you could, at times, spend half the day waiting to fetch the precious commodity. As the number of refugees increased, the people's sense of decency decreased. People took advantage of circumstances and jumped the queue, feeling they were stronger than the rest of us or considered themselves senior members of the camp.

I remember several occasions on which my brothers, sisters and I went to get water, and found ourselves embroiled in family fights with other people. There was a "senior" family, for example, whose members often came for water late and cut in line, notwithstanding that others had been waiting in line for hours.

One day, Farah, a giant from the "senior" family, tried to cut in front of my sister, Fardowsa, my brother Abdirizak and me. I explained to him that I wasn't going to allow that for the simple reason that it was unfair to me and to those behind us in the queue. My hard stance seemed to startle many in the queue, who had somehow come to accept that they were inferior or had lesser rights compared to refugees who had settled in the camp much earlier.

"What's the worst thing you can do about that?" he asked.

"I am going to report you to the security office."

"Let's see if you can do that, and I will crush your face as your beautiful sisters watch, and they will fall for me." He had hardly finished his threats before Abdirizak, and Fardowsa started yelling at him, telling him to watch out.

Farah yelled back at Abdirizak and kicked his jerry can off the queue. Abdirizak gave Farah a hard kick in the belly, before Farah responded with a flying kick that got Abdirizak's nose bridge, triggering profuse bleeding. I wasn't going to watch my brother go down, so I joined the fight, kicking, punching, slapping and biting a stubborn Farah, who seemed not to notice what I was doing. Thank goodness, Ismail, an older neighbor at the camp, decided he was going to stop Farah; and stop Farah he did, in the kind of fashion that only Farah could understand.

I guess he must have hit the bully between his legs, since I can't imagine how a simple kick could send Farah rolling and writhing on the ground with so much pain. Ismail was not done with Farah, but Abdirizak and Fardowsa stopped him, reassuring him that what he had done was enough to teach the brute a lesson. After a short while, we got our jerry cans full of water and headed home.

But we hadn't gone far before Abdirizak, Fardowsa, Ismail and I were rounded up by security officers and taken to the police post at the camp's front entrance. We were given a stern warning never to engage in scuffles again; else we would become guests of the state. The four of us tried explaining to the three officers that we weren't the ones at fault—we were only defending ourselves from aggression. No one listened. The officer who had brought us in only responded: "You should never take the law into your own hands, report to us if you have any such problems."

Limited access to water meant that sanitation was a major issue at Utange. Although there should have been at least one latrine per family, there must have been one such facility per ten families. This meant that at times you couldn't use the facility when you needed it most, and often you would have to swallow your pride and squat in a nearby bush.

When it rained, all that had been hidden in the bush would be brought right to people's doorsteps by the surface runoffs. Bathing was a hallowed activity, now that bathrooms were as scarce as latrines. To take a bath, you had to wake up early before anyone else. There was no running water—warm or cold. We had to use our meager rations of drinking water for other needs as well.

Though I had loved school back in Mogadishu, what I had witnessed in the past few months had quenched any craving I earlier had for education. I had even lost track of what grade I now should have been in, for the camp ran a completely different system of education compared to Somalia.

There was one small, overcrowded tent that served as a school at the camp. Most of the teachers were volunteers. Due to the shortage of resources, there were no specific grades, so children in the same age group were lumped together and taught the same thing at one corner of the tent, while a different class took place at a distant corner or outside the tent. Mostly, we learned English, mathematics and Swahili.

I enrolled at the camp school for just a few weeks and then dropped out. Learning here wasn't as fun as it had been in Mogadishu, mainly because classes were taught in English and Swahili, languages that were new to me. My interest thus stayed with playing soccer, which, I reasoned, I could do whether I went to class or not. So I did not make much use of the educational opportunity that I had at the camp.

I was later to regret this missed opportunity upon coming to the United States, where I discovered that people who had attended the language classes at the camp coped much better with life, as they could freely express themselves in English. Someone like me, who had played soccer when I should have been learning, needed assistance from interpreters on a daily basis to communicate. As I will discuss in later chapters, I had to work harder at learning English in order to survive in the United States. I was thus enrolled into an after-school program. I had to befriend mainstream Americans and spend more time in the library studying the English language.

**Second-Class Refugees**
The daily routine for most of us at the camp revolved around us boys going to the main Utange camp to socialize. Those who had accepted schooling would proceed to class, while those with a different view of life, like me, headed to the field to play soccer. Girls mostly remained at home cooking for the family, although they could also visit each other's abodes to chat and socialize.

Indigenous Kenyan communities around Utange camp did not fancy the idea of having refugees living among them. This was mainly because the camp had sprung up and grown too fast, putting a great strain on the area's resources. The indigenous communities felt that their opinions should have been sought before the government decided to bring foreigners to live in the area.

Consequently, there were many instances of open hostility visited upon the refugees by the local Giriama community and any mistreatment meted out to a refugee was generally not viewed as a crime. At local centers, refugees would at times be charged more than locals for the same kind of item or service. There seemed to be a notion that refugees were mobile ATM machines, especially among the local police officers. They would come out to hunt for "ATMs" after dark. Any refugees finding themselves outside the camp would be arrested, notwithstanding their age, gender or the reason for being out. Once arrested, only the coughing up of some cash would set one free. It is no wonder that time and time again the Kenyan police have topped the charts as being the most corrupt institution in Africa.

With the growing tensions between the locals and refugee community at Utange, there were periodic scuffles involving the Giriamas and the refugees. When such matters reached the law enforcement agencies, Somalis almost always were convicted as guilty of aggression. They would then be locked up in police cells and later released in "out-of-court settlements."

One day, matters boiled over and what we had all long feared, happened. I can't remember the actual event that triggered the conflict, but I recall one mid-afternoon when our small village on the fringes of the main Utange camp was attacked. I had just returned home, tired from playing soccer. I was fortunate that we had some water left from the previous day, so I headed to the bathroom.

Shortly after, my sister Fardowsa came home very frightened. "Are you okay, what happened?" Mom enquired.

"The Giriamas are attacking us refugees. Hussein's family has been attacked. I just came from Yasmin's house. The attackers are using machetes on people."

Everyone gathered around a corner of our home, frightened. Wali, who had returned from the main camp just before me, calmed everyone. "We need to first of all find out what is happening so that we can take the right actions." However, even before he had finished his sentence, my cousin Abdikani arrived from the main camp.

"The fighting is large-scale.... I came to tell you we must flee to safety as soon as possible!" he said, adding :"Our cousin Abdi has been slashed several times with machetes, I don't know his condition. My friends and I were chased down. Get out, Giriamas are heading this way!"

Just then, there was a loud voice, "Get out of my country, you blood-thirsty people!" We panicked. Running out wasn't perhaps the wisest thing to do at that point as the attackers had already come upon our shelters. No one moved. The commotion intensified outside, with desperate screams amidst war chants and curses. We could hear the sound of houses catching fire, and desperate cries of children left behind by their fleeing parents in the ensuing confusion. Everyone got busy doing what had proved to work for us in such moments of crises; praying.

Suddenly there was a recognizable voice calling from outside: "Wali, Wali, you are safe, don't worry." It was Salim, a Giriama friend from the neighborhood. "I have pleaded with the attackers and told them your family is an exception, you are good people," he continued. Mom reached out for Wali's hand.

"We have seen this before, don't believe him. It's a shrewd attempt to get us to open the door so they can finish us too," she cautioned.

"Wali, I am guarding your door, no one will touch you. Just calm down, you're safe," came Salim's voice once again. He sounded convincing. Wali felt he needed to respond, if only to strengthen Salim's desire to be our guardian angel.

"Salim, you know we have been good friends. We fled from war in our country to have a chance in life. We are innocent and we have never caused any problem. As good human beings, we need your protection today," he implored.

"Once again, Wali, remain assured of your safety. I am here and am not leaving till this madness is over," said Salim.

We remained indoors for another 45 minutes or so. We then heard a voice coming from a public address system: "This is a message from the Red Cross. If you are refugees living in this area, please come out. We have trucks ready to evacuate you and your families." The voice went on and on. There was sound of a helicopter making rounds above, sounding quite close overhead.

It was Wali who stood up first and went to open the door. He drew back the latch, pulled the door open and stepped out. My sister Hana, Abdirizak and I followed him. Salim was standing a few meters away, scanning the extent of the damage. There were broken cooking utensils, clothes, jerry cans, basins and personal effects strewn all over the compound. There was smoke billowing from the houses that had been set on fire and there was no one attempting to put out the fires. The place resembled a wasteland. The sight was horrifying, so we returned to our home's front yard.

We found Wali waving at an approaching white truck owned by the Red Cross and the driver signaled that he was coming over. We dashed back to the house, collected our belongings and wrapped them up in bed sheets. There was no time to pack things in suitcases, we heaved what we could onto our backs and went to meet the approaching truck. The destination was Utange main camp, the very same place where we had earlier on been unable to get a place to set up a tent.

Our arrival at the camp was met with a mild degree of resistance by fellow refugees who felt that, because of the crisis, we should have bargained for a better deal than simply accepting to be placed in an already congested camp. They feared we had come to stretch the meager resources available even thinner. Thus our fellow refugees categorized us as second-class refugees.

Second-class refugee status meant that at times we didn't have the same access to resources as original refugees. This new status was made worse, because while earlier on we had had a relatively well-built house outside the camp, now we were back to living in tents as we had earlier done in Dadaab. Worse still, since all good places had already been taken up, the little space that my family got to set up tents was on low-lying land. That meant that while the rest of the country prayed for rain, we had a different prayer, lest we got swept away by floods from the higher grounds.

The worst pinch that I felt from being a second-class refugee was at the soccer pitch. While we had earlier on played the game without regard for anyone's status, now I realized that I the other boys and I, who had recently moved into the main camp had fewer rights. We were no longer guaranteed places in our respective teams. What's more, available fields were "owned" by respective teams, so there were no places for us to play soccer. Whatever team I approached, declined to take me in despite my obvious talent.

Deprived of any opportunity to play, I got bored and remained stuck in our small tent. There were many others like me who had moved into the camp and were suffering the same fate as me. There was Malik, Hassan and Ahmed among others, who were my age mates and loved soccer like I did. We felt enough was enough; we had to assert our rights to play the game we loved.

We summoned up our courage, formed our own team and then confronted the teams that had "owned" the communal soccer fields.

This time around it wasn't going to be a match contest, but a fistfight to force our way into the pitch to play. That seemed the only way to assert ourselves and get our rights respected. We did this about three times before the elders intervened and helped us the same access to soccer space as everyone else.

Life in the camps eventually proved unbearable for most of my family members. There were such frequent outbursts of anger that we feared losing our minds. Depression was getting quite common too, with the prolonged uncertainty about the future. The most affected person was Dad, who needed urgent treatment for complications arising from acute depression and severe backache. While a backache was something about which he had complained from time to time even back in Somalia because of his long working hours, the problem had worsened as a result of the long journeys we made along bad roads while escaping the fighting back in Mogadishu.

Depression was a new phenomenon, as was high blood pressure, and both were getting worse by the day. As a result, the Red Cross recommended that my family be relocated to Nairobi, Kenya's capital city, where we could get easier access to medical help. Thus my family moved to the Eastleigh district of Nairobi.

# Part 2

# America Here I Come

# Chapter 5
## Coming to America

Waiting for peace to return to Somalia so that we could return to normal life in Mogadishu was like waiting for Godot. We had done everything humanly possible to while the time away. We had played football at the camp in Utange, fought with Giriamas, sang our rich Somali folk songs, walked around and about, sat under the trees, exchanged all the riddles and proverbs we knew, all in the hope that a voice would suddenly come calling that it was time to return home.

There were times the fighting in Somalia would subside and peace talks would begin. Those were the happiest times in our lives as refugees, and the joy brought about by the prospects of going home soon was at times too emotional. We would each celebrate such moments at home with silent tears of joy. But then suddenly news would emerge that the peace talks had collapsed. Fierce fighting would once again break out and the hope of peace returning to our motherland would evaporate.

By September of 1991 the factions fighting for supremacy in Mogadishu had increased from the initial United Somali Congress (USC), which significantly contributed to Siyad Barre's ouster from power, to number about five. The USC had already split into two factions one led by Ali Mahdi Muhammad, who had by now risen to become Somali's interim president, and the other led by Mohamed Farah Aideed.

With so many different opposition groups controlling different parts of the country, violence had touched almost all corners of Somalia, many times a deliberate targeting of the civilian population. The most disturbing thing about the conflict was the fact that the factional leaders failed to recognize and respect the mandate of international humanitarian organizations that had come to assist the innocent civilians caught up in the conflicts. In many instances, the factions blocked all access routes to the interior of Somalia, stole relief supplies and at times even killed aid workers. As a result of reduced farming and other economic activities, as well as fierce drought that affected the country, it is estimated that an estimated 300,000 Somalis died of starvation between 1991 and 1992.

Some scholars argue that life under Somali warlords who often mobilized clan-based militias into violence against civilians was worse than life under dictator Siyad Barre.

The effects of the power and leadership vacuum that resulted from Barre's ouster have been the suffering of the masses and crumbling of the state of Somalia. As a result, the majority of Somali children have remained uneducated and malnourished,  and Somalia's elderly population is scattered across the globe, longing for the big day when they'll return to a country they can call their own.

As the armed fighting in Somalia dragged on, we became increasingly convinced as a family that we needed an alternative and more definite plan for settling down and beginning life afresh. Though hopeful of returning home, we nonetheless wanted to be pragmatic. My elder brothers and sisters needed better jobs to earn a living. The younger members of my family, including myself, needed education so as to prepare for life in the future. Mom and Dad, as they grew older, deserved a better place than a refugee camp to which to retire.

Given the high number of people seeking asylum in Kenya from countries such as Rwanda, Burundi, Sudan, Ethiopia, Zaire (Democratic Republic of Congo DRC) and now Somalia, it had become very difficult for refugees to acquire Kenyan citizenship and resettle in the country. Had this been possible, it would perhaps have offered us an opportunity to find a place to live and start a business in Nairobi, with the help of our relatives and friends.

We would also have pursued education in a country where we were more familiar with its people and their ways of life. Being closer to Somalia would have also helped us keep hopes of peace and possible return to Mogadishu alive. But these were just hopes. No matter how much we tried, we couldn't secure Kenyan citizenship. From our assessment of what we wanted to do as a family, no other country in the region provided as good prospects as Kenya.

As mom and dad discussed the matter with Yusuf, my elder half-brother living and working in the United States at the time, they decided that he would look into the possibility of us relocating to the United States as refugees.

So Yusuf approached the Church World Service in Denver with a request to have us sponsored for immigration.

This promise seemed to light a candle of hope in our life as a family. We felt that even though our path had been dark and treacherous, God still had good plans for us, so we kept praying for the plan's success. This was so far the nearest hope we had of ever living a normal life again.

However, the worst tragedy of my life was to happen about three weeks after moving to Eastleigh in Nairobi. Dad, who had been ailing from high blood pressure and unexplained terrible lower back pains since leaving Mogadishu, unfortunately died in 1993.

In accordance with Muslim practice, dad was laid to rest on the same day he died, at a Muslim cemetery. The week that followed my dad's death was one of the lowest moments in my life. We mourned with just a handful of relatives, fellow believers with whom we worshipped at the mosque and people who had come to know us in the EastLeigh neighborhood.

Losing the family's pillar and the greatest hero there ever was in our life as a family, shook us all. It created a void in my heart, a kind of hollowness that I couldn't explain.

There wasn't an autopsy done to confirm the cause of his death. The fact that he had suffered a myriad of health complications seemed to suffice.

Though my father had been ailing, his presence had provided the reassurance we had needed in life. He had been a big part of my life, and I knew he felt the same about me, my mom, and my brothers and sisters. Nothing illustrates the significance of my father's life to me more than the fact that his blood still flows in my veins.

I will forever remain grateful to my brother Wali, who once again rose to the occasion and provided the leadership we needed as a family to navigate through the tragedy. He kept comforting us, saying that, as sad as the situation was, "God had seen it fit to call Dad home because he had fought his earthly battles well." True, dad had given us all the support we needed to make it through the remaining part of our voyage to a happier and more fulfilling life.

He had given us the best kind of foundation and hadn't spared money or effort to see my elder siblings obtain a quality education. He had supported Mom in her business back in Mogadishu. He had done whatever had been within his powers to make things better for his family. So when Wali reminded us all that dad's passing on was God's will and that God's intention was not to just take dad away and leave us suffering, I knew that was the truth. This gave me confidence to start my life again with a greater determination to live.

## The Visa Interview

If you were born and brought up in the United States, you might never understand the rigors of the process that a foreigner goes through to get the chance to live in this country. The immigration process is a strict affair and the scrutiny is even more intense for immigrants coming from a war-torn region such as the Horn of Africa.

A major reason for this kind of strictness has been the American government's zeal to fight terrorism across the globe. It is known that terrorism training thrives in countries with weak institutions of governance. By that time, Somalia's institutions of governance were not just weak, they had been run down completely and it was a land of "every man for himself and God for us all."

With this state of affairs, there were several identifiable terrorism cells in Somalia, mainly training camps for terrorists, both domestic and global.

Later in 1998, terrorists believed to have been co-ordinating their activities from Somalia, attacked the American embassies in Nairobi–Kenya and Dar es Salaam in Tanzania. The attackers were believed to be members of the al-Qaida network.

The effort of getting us sponsorship from Church World Service in Denver, Colorado, was one part of the equation. The second part was the screening process at the Joint Voluntary Agency (JVA) in Nairobi.

JVA handles the U.S. refugee resettlement program in Eastern and Southern Africa through a Cooperative Agreement with the Department of State/Bureau of Population, Refugees and Migration. The body is also responsible for the preparation of refugee case files for adjudication by what was then called Citizenship and Immigration Services (CIS) officers, as well as the out-processing of all approved cases. Today, CIS is part of the Homeland Security Department.

In Kenya, JVA matters, back then as they are today, are administered by Church World Service and is based in Nairobi.

JVA had received our application for immigration to the United States as refugees and the request had passed the preliminary stages. Good news—we were informed of our scheduled interviews at the organization's offices in Nairobi about a month in advance. The purpose of the interview was to ascertain the genuineness of our status.

We had heard many tales about how tense the exercise was and how the interviewers could look right into your eyeballs and read your mind. People who had been through the process told us that interviews for Somali nationals were being conducted by the CIA and the FBI to screen out and arrest anyone who had ever come into contact with gun powder. No criminal or person who had shed innocent blood in what had now become senseless war in Somalia would be allowed into the United States.

Word was that there were lie detectors trained on the interviewees in the interview rooms and they would relay signals to Washington each time you blinked or hesitated to answer a question—indicators that you were telling half-truths or outright lies. This would lead to automatic disqualification from ever setting your foot on U.S. soil. We dreaded this.

Though none of us in the family had touched gun powder, engaged in crime or killed anything save for cows and goat for food, we didn't want anyone to fail the interview as we couldn't imagine leaving anyone of us behind.

So we rehearsed for the interview almost each day. We role-played and fired the craziest of questions that we thought the interviewers could ask.

The person being questioned had to provide comprehensive answers, no matter how awkward the question was. A typical rehearsal session at home would proceed like this:

Mom: "Tell us, Mr. Wali, why do you think it's important for you and your family to move to the United States."

Wali: "We have been on the run from war in Somalia and refugee status in Kenya doesn't allow us to live to our greatest potential. My family and I thus feel we stand a better chance at starting over our lives again by immigrating to the U.S."

Mom: "You have no documents on you as proof of any professional training. How do you think the U.S. will benefit from having you as an immigrant over there?"

Wali: "You see I might not be an expert in engineering or other highly regarded fields. I am nonetheless willing to start off at the bottom of the ladder. By working as a care giver, taxi driver, dish washer or whatever job that I will get, I will have contributed to making the services available to Americans at an affordable cost."

Mom: "You don't have a wife as yet. When do you hope to marry, who do you hope to marry, and how many children do you intend to bear on American soil?"

Wali: "Now this is mom talking, not the interviewer...."

Fardowsa: "Hey gentleman, can you answer the question!"

On the appointed day for the interview, Wednesday, March 10, 1993, the entire family of fourteen boarded the red and white Stage Coach bus at Eastleigh headed to Nairobi's city centre. It was 6:30 a.m. when we arrived at the JVA office in Nairobi.

Like everyone else with scheduled appointments that morning, we queued outside the building's main gate waiting for the official opening hours so we could be ushered in.

The gates opened at 8:00 a.m. and we walked into the lobby. Like most of my family members, it was my first time ever at an immigration interview. The lobby was a medium-sized hall, well ventilated and with cozy black seats. It had large clear windows and the sun lit up the room. The lighting was accentuated by the white fluorescent lights tucked away in the ceiling. You could hear the sound of the morning traffic on the city street. The atmosphere seemed to ease the nervousness that we felt as we walked in.

We took our seats in the lobby and waited for further instructions. The interview had been scheduled for 9 a.m., but we had rationalized that it would be to our benefit if we got there way ahead of time. This would give us time to familiarize ourselves with the environment and possibly help us to manage our nervousness. We hoped we could bump into fellow Somalis coming from the interview who could at least give us an idea of how the immigration sessions were being conducted.

Ready as we might have been for the interview, we nonetheless felt nervous about one subtlety. Save for the alien ID cards and a letter of introduction from the UNHCR office in Nairobi, we didn't have any other documents on us. We didn't have birth certificates or any verifiable proof that we were actually born in Somalia. Our only saving grace was the letter from the UNHCR, which had indicated the date we crossed the border into Kenya. The letter stated too that we had been residents of Dadaab and Utange refugee camps in Kenya.

Truth is, we had left most of our belongings including our birth certificates and academic transcripts at home in Mogadishu during our escape from the fighting in the city. We had lost even more of what we carried during our long journey of zigzagging across Somalia's battlefields on our way to the Liboi boarder with Kenya. The only precious things we had managed to cross the border into Kenya with were our souls, and that's what we had brought to the interview.

At a quarter to nine, the lady at the registration desk signaled Wali to come over. He did and they conversed for a few moments, then he came back.

"She wanted to know our dates of birth, since these had been left blank on all the forms she had with her. I explained that we didn't have our birth certificates. But the problem has been solved, she has indicated January 1, the year that I gave her for when each one of us was born," he told us.

At that moment we didn't care much about the birthdates that were assigned to us or how she had arrived at the dates. We did not ask because we did not wish to complicate matters; we just shut up and waited for instructions.

This was our first formal collective test as a family. It meant so much to us since failure would mean our hopes and dreams to come to the United States would be doomed.

At exactly nine o'clock, I glanced at my brother Abdirizak scanning through a magazine. He appeared composed, as opposed to the guy who had woken up completely nervous and sweating all over just a few hours before. He seemed ready to face the test. Finally we were invited into the interview room. We glanced at each other as if checking if we accepted our common fate.

Wali, who was leading the way, suddenly stopped and turned back. "Guys, hear me out! Do not speak unless you are asked to. Do not project any signs of nervousness. Our future depends on how well we express ourselves in this session, so let me do most of the talking." He was our leader; we respected and trusted him because he had been through more in life than most of us.

We were ushered into a small boardroom by the lady at the registration desk. There was a large brown table in the middle of the room with fifteen seats arranged along the length and width of the table. We took our seats, and for strategic reasons, Wali sat at the farthest edge of the room, directly overlooking the seats that we hoped the interviewers would occupy. Speaking from that far edge would create an impression that all of us were actively participating in the proceedings, even though we had Wali as our spokesperson.

Two minutes after settling down, the doorknob turned and in came two women dressed in black trousers and white blouses, and one wore a pair of thin-rimmed eyeglasses. They each held in their hands a folder and a bunch of keys. They greeted us and settled on the seats that we had left for them and introduced themselves.

"Welcome to the immigration interview. The main objective of this session is not to deny you an opportunity to immigrate to the United States. We just want to ascertain that your intentions are genuine. We also want to find out how much assistance you will need in order to settle down fast and begin your life afresh in a faraway country. But some word of caution here please, only genuine and deserving cases can go through. So relax, enjoy the interaction and above all, we know you will be as truthful in your responses as you possibly can," said the bespectacled lady in a friendly yet upfront tone.

Rather than relax, we seemed to get more anxious. We exchanged glances across the room, trying to digest the import of those words. However, deep within us we knew that our case was genuine. All we needed now was to prove this to the interviewers in whose hands our fate lay. By the stroke of a pen, they could dim or brighten our dreams of starting life again in America.

"Ms. Seed (Mom), we would wish to confirm whether these are the family members with whom you wish to immigrate to the U.S. Am I correct?" said the bespectacled interviewer.

"Yes, madam, you're correct."

The interviewer then proceeded to read our names as each of us responded in the affirmative.

"Why did you leave your home in Somalia, Ms. Seed?"

"We left home after our neighborhood was attacked by fighters. It was no longer safe to stay there, especially with the children. We fled to Afgoye, which unfortunately sank into war, and later Kismayu, which too went under. Our only chance was to find our way into Kenya in order to escape from the fire back home."

"Mr. Wali, What do you think would happen if your family returned to Somalia now?"

"If we went back to Somalia, chances are we wouldn't go far past the border with Kenya before we are either killed, or forcefully recruited into the factional armies. Still, I am not sure we would find our former home intact. We lived in an up-scale neighborhood with several influential people in Siyad Barre's government and by now the houses would not have been spared by the fighters and looters. In short, we wouldn't have a place to go back to, and chances of losing our lives would be higher compared to chances of surviving."

"Ms. Seed, you're the head of this family, now that I see your husband passed away recently. Please accept our condolences. But why did you choose to apply to go to the United States.?"

"A number of reasons, madam," Mom replied. "First, finding a peaceful place to rebuild our lives is the most import thing for us. Secondly, we need proper health care and economic opportunities, which aren't available in the refugee camps, or are not availed to refugees in Kenya."

The session lasted close to 45 minutes. Only the bespectacled lady spoke, the other just took notes. Finally the interviewer told us that we stood good chances of being resettled to the United States. She added that we only had to go through medical exams in the coming months and if we passed this, then it would be just a matter of time before we bid Africa goodbye.

With all hurdles out of the way now, saying we were excited would be an understatement. We couldn't help but dream of how fast we were going to enroll in good schools, complete our university education and start earning. We vowed to ourselves that given what we had gone through, we weren't going to forget the kinsmen we were leaving behind. They didn't deserve what they were going through and we had not done anything extraordinary for God to bless us with such a great opportunity to transform our lives for the better. We were thus going to use a portion of the "$ millions" that we would be earning in the States to help out our families suffering in Kenya, Ethiopia and Somalia.

## Flight to the land of Hope and Opportunities

After the qualification to immigrate, time moved too fast. The seven months waiting period from July 1993 to the departure date of January 23, 1994 was the shortest of all waiting times I had experienced since leaving Mogadishu. Each day had its own preparations in readiness for the greatest flight in our life. It was going to be a flight from misery to mastery of our own destiny, a flight from anxiety to a life of certainty. It was going to be a flight from the stagnation and confusion that the troubles in Somalia had brought to our lives, to a place where we could plan what to do and wake up to chart a new course of life.

Each day that dawned brought with it a new sense of excitement. For once there seemed to be a genuine end to all the indignities that we had suffered as refugees. In addition, there was true healing from the heartache that we had suffered since leaving our hitherto comfortable life in Medina, Mogadishu.

I was elated at the thought of joining school once more and playing soccer with new friends. The only regret I had was that Dad wasn't going to be with us in our new home in Colorado.

Watching aircraft fly over EastLeigh grew into a near obsession for me. I visualized myself in one headed to the U.S. I would rest on the sofa at home, stretch out my legs as if in a luxurious jet, and order people around to serve us. But that was just the boy in me—I am glad my family understood.

Soon I found myself explaining to my fellow refugees who had also been cleared for immigration to the states, how the pilot accelerates the plane at take off by pressing on the aircraft's gas pedal and how dangerous it can turn out if he slams his foot on the brakes as it would cause the plane to fall off the sky.

I recall arguing with the boys in the neighborhood over whether planes had restrooms and how scary a visit to the restroom would be, as you would be seeing and peeing on the world from up in the sky. We argued over whether there were routes drawn out in the skies which pilots follow to their destination—I hadn't heard yet about autopilot — and whether the pilot can see the ground from up in the sky on a dark rainy night.

We had read books that talked of the four corners of the world; we argued how high one needed to fly to see at least one, if not all the corners. Oh yes, there was also the question of whether we could actually see where the sun comes from in the morning and where it goes in the evening.

These debates would become intense, heated and more exciting especially since they were mainly fueled by our ignorance of matters to do with aviation. To prove our point, it wasn't uncommon for one of us to lie that his or her dad or uncle was a frequent flyer to Mecca, and when on such trips he had made close friends with many pilots. Such arguments were therefore believed to be supported with knowledge from irrefutable sources. The days passed by anyway and finally our big day dawned.

We had spent the past few weeks preparing for the journey. What remained were mainly personal effects such as soap, toothbrushes and toothpaste, shoes and a few clothes. As the day grew closer, Mom developed a generosity streak and started giving things away.

Though selling items such as the sofa set, gas cooker and cylinder, sauce pans, and beds would have afforded us some liquidity with which to spice up life a bit, Mom refused to commercialize our family assets. Therefore, she gave away such items to distant relatives who had somehow found their way to Eastleigh.

January 23, 1994 will forever remain etched in my mind. This was the day we boarded the KLM flight and took off to the skies. There being no direct flights between Kenya and the United States, we left Jomo Kenyatta International Airport (JKIA) in Nairobi headed for Amsterdam. From there we were to board a connecting flight to New York. From New York we were to board an American Airlines flight to Dallas, Texas, before finally heading to Denver, Colorado.

There were several other refugee families from Dadaab and Utange camps lucky to be taking the flight with us to the land of opportunity. There would be a second flight to the States a few days later as more refugees would receive their clearance to immigrate. After the usual clearance at the airport, around 9:30 p.m. we boarded the plane. I was surprised at how big the aircraft was compared to what I was used to seeing up in the sky. I couldn't comprehend just how a machine so big could defy gravity and remain airborne with all the people and luggage onboard. I recall us walking from the departure lounge at JKIA with Wali leading the way carrying a small bag. No one in our nuclear family was left in Kenya. This was going to be our first plane ride ever!

We took our seats. As I watched outside the window, I could see planes landing, and taking off from the airport into the clear night sky. These were spectacular sights that made me long for our takeoff.

About fifteen minutes after checking in, a team of flight attendants came in to conduct the usual demonstration of emergency safety procedures. I followed keenly and it's then I realized the kind of danger we might all be in while flying.

I got the impression that though the instructor had ended the procedures with the words "Enjoy your flight," he knew that there was no guarantee of us getting wherever we were going.

First, I figured there was no way of ensuring that there were no birds in the sky at takeoff—so anything could happen. Second, I wondered whether anyone had checked carefully enough to ensure that the engines wouldn't stall at 39,000 feet above sea level. Third, if the aircraft was to crash on dry land, how were we supposed to go to the wings as per the safety instructor's advice as Wali and Abdirizak interpreted for us, and how was that going to save anyone?

Before I realized what was happening, the plane's engines were revving and the jumbo jet was being pulled in reverse. This gave me a mixed feeling of excitement and fear. Excited to know we had a greater hope ahead of us, but dreading that we were using a far too risky means to get us to the future we had dreamed of for so long.

The bird taxied forward and took a right turn heading for the runway. I watched the two planes ahead of us speed along the long stretch of tarmac and gracefully take off towards the sky. I knew it wasn't going to be long before we, too, were airborne.

After about ten minutes of waiting, the captain's voice came through the intercom. We were getting ready for takeoff. We were to check our safety belts once again. The plane moved on and took another right turn at the far edge of the runway.

I saw Kowsar and Hani, my younger sisters, close their eyes tight as the sound of the engines turned from gentle humming into a roar. I knew I wasn't the only one afraid of the experience—it was a mutual fear that no one was willing to talk about. Soon we were speeding down the runaway. The engines roared on, with the sound and speed changing every few seconds. I enjoyed the cruise, though cautiously listening for any unusual sounds. There were none.

Turning back slightly I saw Mom's contorted face. I had never seen her like that before. I tried to move but felt the belt running across my waist. Looking across the window under the moonlight I saw sparse clouds hanging just over the aircraft. I couldn't believe how fast the ascent had been. Just when did we leave the runway?

The giant machine took a swerve to the left. I feared the tilt. There were some slight shattering sounds as the wings cut through the clouds. Looking through the window I saw how far the ground was. I couldn't even imagine where we now were.

I had hoped to look out and see EastLeigh and perhaps wave at anyone I knew, but the chance was already lost. Suddenly the pilot reduced the bird's engine power after the crucial stage of ascent. This made me feel as though the machine was losing height. It was a bad feeling, like coming down a tall building in a fast-moving elevator. Even if we were overflying Eastleigh and came across anyone I knew, I wasn't sure I was going to let go the seat I was now clinging onto to wave to them.

Then suddenly I heard the captain's voice and Wali's translation came. "We are now flying at 33,000 feet above sea level. We hope to touch down at Schiphol Airport in Amsterdam in the next nine hours. For now you may enjoy a meal...." That was such a long time to hang in the sky; I wondered how calm and composed the captain could be at such a time when my heart was throbbing in my chest.

## Amsterdam Stopover

It was midnight when we landed at Schiphol Airport, Amsterdam. Our scheduled connection flight to New York was eight hours away, so we remained within the airport. Taking a glance at the clock on the wall, I pointed out to Abdirizak that contrary to what the captain had announced in the plane, the flight from Nairobi had actually taken eight hours. He smiled at my ignorance.

"The world has different time zones. Nairobi is +3 hours GMT and Amsterdam is +2 hours GMT.

"That means Amsterdam is one hour behind Nairobi," he explained.

During the hours we waited at the airport, I was amazed by the experience of being in this huge enclosure with all the luxuries: nice chairs and clean bathrooms. We felt tired after the journey but the excitement of being in another part of the world took the better part of us.

Abdirizak and Wali kept an eye over the airport's arrivals and departures notice board lest we miss the connection flight and get stranded in a foreign country.

I forgot to check the exact time we boarded the KLM direct flight to JF Kennedy International Airport in New York, though Wali told us it was going to be another eight hours non-stop of overflying the Atlantic Ocean.

We touched down at JF Kennedy International Airport amidst much darkness. I had already lost track of time. Taking a glance at the airport's lobby, we were surprised to see so much darkness at just 4:30 p.m. We did not know anything about the daylight saving that is observed in the U.S. In the Horn of Africa, the sun rises at around six and sets around six. We had never heard of the clock being propped an hour ahead or backwards depending on the season.

It was January 26 when we arrived at Denver, Colorado. It was a snowy day. I still recall my sister Kowsar, mom and I seated next to each other in the plane from Dallas, wondering what the white stuff covering the ground was. Kowsar insisted that it was salt.

At the airport in Denver, there was Yusuf, his wife Anab, as well as James and Dorothy, from the Church

*Top left: Hamse Warfa at 5 years of age. Right: Just before leaving Nairobi for the US in 1994. Above: Hamse as a leader discussing with Terrano Houston in City Heights.*

World Service in Colorado awaiting our arrival. It was such an emotional moment for us. We headed straight to Yusuf's home. This is where we were to stay for a week as the Church World Service looked for an appropriate place to house fourteen people!

Life at Yusuf's house was amazing. I couldn't help but marvel at the kind of luxury in which he lived. While we had come from a place devoid of hot water for bathing and where we had to line up to fetch drinking water in jerry cans, here there was plenty of clean and safe water running from the taps. In addition, there were microwaves to warm food and a king size refrigerator to keep food cool. Surely this was America!

So many things were unfamiliar. On my cousin's first shower, he couldn't tell which bottle contained lotion. He took one bottle hoping that it contained lotion and applied it all over his body. Since his friends were knocking on the bathroom door, waiting to shower, he quickly appointed himself as their advisor and showed them what he had used. They excitedly did as he had done.

A few minutes later their skin was dry, almost cracking. Save for the decent clothes they wore, they looked like street urchins. Oh my, they had mistaken deodorant for lotion. Not that he had never seen or used lotion before, only that here in America the packaging is more sophisticated. Back in Somalia most of the cosmetics were made from natural ingredients such as flowers and tree barks and the packaging wasn't as important as the content. For my family, a new life in America was about to begin!

# Chapter 6
# Settling Down

After spending a couple of days at home, it was time to get things moving. The first thing we did was to visit the Church World Service office to start our paperwork. We needed to be oriented on how to start off and how to adapt well in the American way of life, as well as get advice on where and how to start schooling— at least for those of us who were still of school age.

However, there was the challenge of having to transport a family of fourteen in Yusuf's small 1985 Toyota Corolla. Owing to this limitation, Church World Service scheduled a total of three separate meetings so we could go in smaller groups.

Our next stop was at the Social Security Administration to apply for Social Security. I had no idea what Social Security was. Back in Somalia this was only mentioned in relation to retiring officers, but hardly did young people have to think about Social Security.

We then proceeded to the County of Denver to apply for welfare benefits, food stamps and medical benefits. Having these documents in our hands, it was time for my elder brothers and sisters to start looking for jobs.

One day, my sister, Fardowsa, requested me to accompany her to the Department of Motorcycle (DMV) so that she could apply for state identification. To Fardowsa, we were acting responsibly and proactively. She figured this would be better than having to wait for someone to take us there.

We decided to take a bus to our destination. Fardowsa believed that her communication skills were sufficient to get us to the DMV for her ID. I was younger than sixteen so I didn't require an ID back then.

We didn't inform anyone what our plans were or where we intended to go. The Department of Motor Vehicles (DMV), which issues the ID cards, was not far from where we lived, but how could we know this without consulting with anyone?

Fardowsa and I innocently thought that the bus would automatically stop when we got to the registration office and announce our arrival. But this did not happen. Instead, we rode the bus for over an hour. Then it came to a stop and it was announced that the bus had gotten to its final destination. As it was, the bus was now expected to head to a different part of the city. All other passengers alighted, but owing to our confusion, we remained seated.

The driver must have sensed our tension because he came up to us and addressed us: "Folks, we are at our final destination." Fardowsa, in her broken English replied: "but where is our place?"

"What do you mean by 'our place,' madam?" asked the driver.

"We need to go to the government building," replied Fardowsa.

"Which government building?"

"Where are we now?" I inquired.

The driver pointed to a map on the sidewall of the bus. "This is Aurora. If you are looking for directions, use this map."

We didn't have the slightest idea of how to use the map. In panic and worrying about what to do next, we disembarked from the bus. We approached a bystander. He looked middle aged, and was dressed in a dark long jacket. "We are looking for the government building to pay for the government ID," said Fardowsa.

Looking at us strangely, the man said, "Sorry, I can't help you."

We approached a young lady, but she evaded us even before we had the chance to introduce ourselves. It then dawned on us that we looked different from everyone else. Here we were, I wearing an oversized suit donated to me by the Church World Service. Fardowsa was wearing her hijab. This was not the kind of clothing for winter. It was obvious to everyone that we were newcomers to America.

After several unsuccessful attempts at finding out where we were or where we could get help, we finally encountered a man who was kind enough to hear us out. After explaining our predicament to him, he said, "I don't understand what you mean by government ID, but if you're looking for a photo center, there is a place two blocks from here." He directed us to the photo center.

When we got to the photo center, Fardowsa made the enquiry, stating, "We need government picture."

The young lady behind the counter scanned us from top to bottom. "Sorry, we don't issue IDs here.

You will have to go to DMV," she explained. Feeling a bit relieved and closer to a solution, Fardowsa went on, "Where is that?"

She directed us to take a bus that was heading in the direction opposite from where we had come from. We took her instructions and sure, we found our way to Denver's DMV. Fardowsa filled out the forms and, Voila! We had made an achievement despite the hiccup!

Upon getting Fardowsa's ID, we walked out of the offices to find a man who resembled us. We guessed he was either Ethiopian or Somali. We approached him and upon enquiry, he confirmed he was Ethiopian. His name was Negasi. We then explained to him our situation (in Amharic language) and what we had gone through. We explained to him that now that we had gotten what we had come for, we didn't know which way home was.

Negasi was so helpful. He seemed to perfectly understand our problem and he was kind enough to ride with us on the bus and he helped us change to another bus that would take us home. After over a twelve hour ordeal, we returned home late in the evening. Everyone at home had already panicked. Wali seemed the most annoyed of them all.

"Where were you guys," he asked angrily.

"Hamse went with me to get an ID," explained Fardowsa, handing it over to Wali. He saw just how thoughtful we had been to try getting such a document. That seemed to cool down everyone's nerves.

"Ok," said Wali. "Next time you should let us know whenever you're going out for long."

**Hunger, Pork and Wine**

Several weeks after settling down in Denver, I was enrolled at South High School. I was initially taken in as an
eighth grader but because of my age I was transferred to
the ninth grade.

In school, my best friend was Alex, a boy of my age
whose family had recently moved to the United States
from Russia. Alex was a forthright boy who, like me, was
facing serious communication challenges as neither of
us spoke English well. Isn't it interesting how human beings develop relationships and form friendships even
in the absence of a common language through which to
communicate?

Attending a school that had an overwhelmingly white
student population made me feel a bit disoriented. My
poor language skills made things even harder for me because I couldn't articulate my ideas well. In fact, for the
first week and a half, I did not come across a student
of color. I felt completely different and lost. This was
nowhere close to the earlier dreams I had harbored of
enrolling in wonderful schools and working hard to be
at the top of my studies. The language and cultural barrier seemed insurmountable. It was hard relating to the
rest of the student population; hence, I spent most of the
time with Alex.

One Friday morning during break time I spotted a
black student. I walked up to him. He too seemed surprised to see another African student at South High
School. I introduced myself as Hamse Warfa from Somalia. "Am Birhanu, from Ethiopia," he replied. As he explained to me later, Birhanu and his family had migrated

to America eight months before us. He was in the tenth grade. Unlike me, Birhanu was a good English speaker, and having been around for a little longer period than us, he was more confident about himself and thus he became my guide.

One of my biggest adjustment challenges in school was food. I still recall that most of the times I left home so early that I hardly had time to have breakfast. After all, I knew there would be something to eat at school.

The breakfast served in school was not bad. It mainly consisted of small cakes, sometimes cereals and orange juice. This was mainly served free of charge to students like me and Birhanu who came from low-income families. Interestingly, few students bothered at all about one's social status, so this didn't make us feel inferior.

But there was lunchtime too. Jetting out of classes so hungry, students would rush to the cafeteria to line up for food. After coming to America, I did not imagine there would ever be another form of queuing to get food. For the few times that I ate at school, I felt that the queues were manageable, as they were not too long and students interacted well as they waited to be served. This was certainly nothing compared to the queues in the refugee camps in Kenya.

The school provided sandwiches for lunch. A serious allegation we had heard when we were coming over to America was that every American meal, no matter how simple, contained pork and wine.

Since our religion forbids consumption of pork and drinking of alcohol, I thus kept off any kind of food whose ingredients weren't overtly declared! I was also very picky on foods. For instance, I did not eat red meat until much later. I also avoided eggs, cheese, mayonnaise, hot sauces, and ketchup, and other condiments.

This meant that I remained hungry most of the time until three o'clock when school would let out and I would leave for home. Interestingly, no one bothered to find out specifically why I wasn't eating much at school. This went on until one day when the cafeteria manager reported the matter to my counselor.

I was summoned into the counselor's office. Her assertion was that not eating enough quantities of nutritious food had a direct link to my academic performance. This was something the school's administration was getting concerned about. I was going to be referred to a doctor who would check on my health before I could be allowed back to class.

I came to my defense: "Before being cleared to come over here, we went through enough medical checkups and we were certified as being 100 percent healthy." But since I never mentioned anything to do with my religion's prohibition of the consumption of pork, there wasn't any confirmation that pork wasn't served in school. So, the status quo remained.

The counselor was baffled; she hadn't expected any response from the seemingly defenseless boy. I guess she had intended to use the medical checkup as a threat, to make taking meals seem like the lesser evil. That hadn't worked. She asked me to return to class with a promise to call me back to look into the matter further. She never called back. In my ignorance and presumption that the food served in school was full of pork, I kept going hungry, while I could have just confirmed the matter and gotten assistance.

Over the year that my family and I were in Denver, I hardly ever took lunch in school. Sometimes I would carry some pastries and fruits from home, but I often finished them before lunchtime, and I remained wishing there was something more to sink my teeth into the rest of the day.

In order to speed up my academic and language skills, I was enrolled in ESL classes. These were evening classes where we got specialized attention from tutors, making learning more fun and easier than in normal daytime classes. Most of my classmates in these lessons were fellow immigrants, mainly from Russia and Mexico.

With the progress that I was making in communication, I came to like schooling. I developed the confidence to chat with strangers and I realized just how easy making new friends was becoming.

I developed a new layer of confidence in my personality and I could now switch from playing soccer to playing basketball. I must admit that many of my friends prevailed upon me on this decision, as they kept telling me: "Wow, you are tall, you should play basketball." Once I got into the basketball court, I discovered that I couldn't resist the charm of the game, more so the team spirit.

### The Two Sides of Life in Denver

Upon getting to Denver, our initial stay was at Lakewood, Colorado. This was a predominantly white community where we hardly saw any person of color. Later, we moved to Denver, but we were still the only Muslim, black and African family in the area. My sisters drew quite a lot of attention for wearing the hijab, which was alien attire to the community in the neighborhood. Mom often wore kanga, a kind of clothing popular among women living along the East African coast, while my brothers and I sometimes wore kitenge, attire common with African men.

Our stay here was received with mixed reaction. Some of our neighbors were kind and would greet us whenever we met. Others offered us food as a show of their welcome and hospitality to us. Dave, a boy of my age, often invited us for a game of basketball at their court, which gave us a good way to interact and pass time in the evenings and over the weekends.

There were also Dorothy and James, wonderful souls from the Church World Service. These two people offered enormous support to our family in helping us settle in and feel comfortable in our new home. Dorothy would come almost on a weekly basis to take us around Denver visiting shopping malls and we would later return home with wonderful presents. I might never get to know how much the dear lady spent on us, especially the fresh fruits she brought with her which were enough to feed the entire family. I am not sure if she was an employee or a volunteer of World Church Services.

It was Dorothy who got us an ESL teacher, who would visit us at home after school to teach us English. I recall our high school English teacher, Valarie, telling me, "Hamse, try to learn at least several new words per day." In the morning, I went to school feeling like a genius, now that I was loaded with a few new English words.

I still recall my first pair of sneakers, which was bought by James. He had taken particular interest in helping me and my family feel at home in Denver. He also brought me a few pairs of sports shoes, basketball jerseys and a basketball.

What surprised me the most about James was that he would leave everything else he was doing just to come and play basketball with us. This was unlike many busy American adults who rarely had the time to spend in sports. Interesting, it was James who brought me my first Gatorade. Boy, wasn't it tasty!

After two months of searching for a job, lady luck finally smiled at my brother Wali. He had casually visited the local McDonald's fast food restaurant for a quick bite. After placing his order, Wali approached a cashier who looked friendly, with the intention of getting to know her better. She informed him that she and a few of her colleagues were Ethiopians.

It is then that Wali explained to them his frustration at not having anything meaningful to do since coming to America. One of the cashiers pulled out a business card from his wallet and handed it to Wali. "Call this number, she's my boss. She is Ethiopian too, maybe she could help," said the cashier.

Excited about the prospect of finding a job, Wali left the restaurant and immediately called the manager. She asked him to fill out an application form, then to come back for an interview later in the week.

A few weeks after the encounter with the manager, the home phone rang at around 9:30 a.m. It was a job offer for Wali! It was jubilation at home as Wali became the first member of the team with which we had immigrated, to secure employment. But things were about to get better.

Upon reporting for duty, Wali, in his characteristic leadership personality, didn't shy off from inquiring whether more such opportunities existed for his siblings. To his surprise, the boss answered in the affirmative. Immediately Wali called home, asking my brother Abdirizak to go and fill in job application forms at the McDonald's. In less than a few weeks, my brothers Wali and Abdirizak  were working. And in that summer of 1994, , I too joined the workforce at McDonald's.

The most interesting thing with our new jobs was that they were in areas considered not typical male jobs in our Somali culture. Traditionally, Somali men do not engage in domestic chores such as cooking or doing the laundry. But since we needed the money to survive and to create our financial independence from the reliance on social welfare, we didn't have the luxury of choosing jobs.

Being their first time working in a kitchen, my brothers had their fair share of goofs. The most ridiculous of them all was me, working closely with Wali in making scrambled eggs at McDonald's. Wali asked me to break the eggs in readiness for cooking. I broke the eggs, poured the yolk into the trashcan and brought the shells to Wali. I had no clue of what was expected of a cook.

"Where are the eggs?" Wali inquired, "I thought what was inside was trash," I replied, innocently.

## Space, Dogs and Time

One of the first cultural differences I noticed upon coming to Denver was at a visit to the grocery store. I had never seen such a huge space with nothing but food! My first exposure was the personal space in the aisles as people walked around shopping.

Whereas, I came from a culture where there is minimum space and it is not unusual for people to rub shoulders as they go about their business, I noticed that here there was a concept known as "personal space." For the first few encounters, I kept getting too close to people, at times touching their shoulders or arms. This was perfectly normal in Africa, but it earned me strange looks whenever this happened. I kept ignoring the disapprovals for weeks until Wali explained to me that I needed to give people their space.

Another cultural shock was learning to talk softly and with minimal gestures. In my culture, we often spoke loudly and with wide hand gesticulations. This is what we did at home and we would later take it to school in my early days. It is simply how we had grown up, but it was something that is not a custom in America.

Talking loudly was often misinterpreted as a sign of anger, and our hand gestures were likewise being perceived as warnings of impending violent consequences. Could this have been the reason why colleagues often frowned at us, even during friendly discussions in school?

Another difference I noted was how valued pets, especially dogs, are in Western societies. Here, I found out that dogs are fed on special meals, they live in the same house as the owner and they often have an attendant to take care of them.

Back home, dogs were the least dignified creatures. They were fed on leftovers and bones and they were never allowed inside the house. In my culture, a dog had no other purpose than providing security.

A major difference I encountered between my African culture and the American lifestyle was in relation to time. In our culture, like many other societies, time is an elastic concept that can be stretched and bent around to fit within different purposes. As such, when we scheduled a meeting back home, reference to time was often an approximation, something like, "Let's meet around noon." This could mean anywhere between 11:30 and 1:00 p.m." Fixing a meeting "after Asr prayer" would mean anywhere between 3 and 5 p.m.

Here in America, I discovered that time was a concise and exact concept. If I had an appointment at, say, noon, that meant it had to be precisely twelve o'clock! Time management is therefore an issue many immigrants continue to struggle with.

In spite of the good reception we had gotten in Denver, not everything proceeded smoothly. For instance, I will never forget this particular day when my brother Abdirizak and I went to play basketball at the neighborhood court after school.

As we were warming up, eight boys of about our age from the neighborhood asked to join in for a full-court match. We agreed to play with them in a good natured gesture.

Two of the boys would from time to time shout words that we didn't understand, though from the tone we suspected they must have been obscenities. We didn't give them much attention although they would shout each time Abdirizak or I got the ball.

Things got worse and the boys started pulling my hands off the ball each time it was my turn to play. They were doing the same to Abdirizak too, pushing him around. This kind of play was only directed towards us.

As the rough game continued, I couldn't take it any longer. I had the ball and one of the boys intentionally pushed me. "Stop it, you stupid!" I shouted at the boy in broken English. For that I got a good punch in my face, which almost brought me down. Abdirizak couldn't watch this happen; he got hold of the boy and gave him a hard knock in the belly. Two more  opponents joined in and jumped into the furor.  We got into a brawl and by the time we got home you couldn't help but notice the bruises developing on our faces and arms.

**A Car at Last!**

One of the most exciting moments in our family came when we purchased a family car. It was a used Toyota Camry that we had all made contributions to purchase, especially Abdirizak who contributed most of the funding. We had gotten tired of walking to the bus stop and using public transport every day, sometimes under the worst of weather conditions. Moreover, we felt that we needed to relieve Dorothy of her weekly trips to the grocery to bring us fruits. We wanted to be able to procure the fruits from the groceries ourselves and virtually be able to go anywhere else we desired.

After having been in the United States for close to a year, Abdirizak had learned how to drive. He had obtained his driver's license and was thus designated as the family's chauffer. For Wali, although he had been driving for more than 20 years in Africa, he was to discover that driving in the U.S. was a completely different ball game. The traffic rules were different and so were the weather conditions and the directions. While in Kenya and Somalia he had driven right hand vehicles keeping to the left, in the U.S. it was a left hand vehicle keeping to the right.

An achievement as it was for us to have bought a car within a year of our coming to the States, this was not a welcome idea to some people in our neighborhood. It seemed that they would have wanted us to do some more walking and continue relying on welfare support.

Whenever we parked the vehicle outside the house, we noticed a flat tire almost every morning. At first we took this as a casual happenstance, especially given that we had bought a pre-owned vehicle. We would get the problem fixed, inflate the tire once again and get onto the road on our way to work.

But then we noticed that the problem would shift to a different tire. In about a week, we had mended all the tires, and we were back to the front right tire, where the problem had started. It then dawned on us that this was not a normal problem—there must be someone playing dirty tricks on us. We then kept vigil to see who could be responsible for the punctures. We realized that on the days we kept popping out through the night at random the tires remained intact. But the days we remained indoors the entire night, we would discover a flat tire in the morning.

The problem, however, took a new twist when we woke up one morning to find a knife dropped next to the rear flat tire. There was a note too, strategically held into place by the wipers against the windshield. On the note was inscribed the following words: "Go back to your country, Niggers!" This was very frightening, especially to my mother who was alone at home most of the time.

We reported the matter to the police. We didn't have any suspects as yet. The police said they would investigate, though we never saw any of them near our home. Luckily, the frequency with which we got flat tires decreased.

Concerns over my mother's isolation in a neighborhood that was increasingly becoming unfriendly, coupled with our difficulties adjusting to school life, spurred us into exploring how we could leave Denver for a safer and more diverse city. We were especially scouting for a place where there wouldn't be much snow and, also, where we could find people from Somalia so that my mother could find people to relate to.

We left this duty mainly to my mother who had more time on her hands to make enquiries during the day. In the evening, we took time to evaluate the options of the places she had discovered. Mom contacted several friends and relatives across the United States. We got invitations to neighborhoods in Seattle, Washington; Minneapolis, Minnesota and Nashville, Tennessee among other cities. We brainstormed the implications of moving, including the distance, cost and opportunities for work and school.

Meanwhile, we kept experiencing the flat tires. Then an incident happened that became the straw that broke the camel's back. It was on a Thursday evening, just as we were having dinner. There was a loud bang, then the glass from the living room window shattered, and a rock hit the table on which food was being served.

This was the scariest experience for us so far since moving to the United States, but thank God no one was hurt. We immediately called the police, who responded very quickly. We had no suspects or witnesses, so it was a weak case from the start.

Early in the next morning, as my sister, Hani, was going about her preparations for school, she decided to take a peek outside through the broken window. That's when she saw a teen from our next door neighbor's house walking towards our car. He squatted next to the rear left wheel, searched inside his black jacket's pocket and drew out what looked like a screwdriver. On seeing the streak of light coming from the slightly drawn curtain from where Hani was peeping, the young man hurriedly returned the tool to his pocket, jumped up and hastily retreated into his house.

The "Aha" moment had come. We reported this to the police. At last we had the suspect. The police came over the following evening and went to the boy's home for questioning. We didn't follow up the matter beyond that, as we had already made up our minds to move from the neighborhood for good. Just like the bombing of Ifrah's home back in Mogadishu, the attack on our house was the sign we had been waiting for to know it was time to move.

After weighing the various options that we had for relocation, San Diego became our ideal destination. To start with, the city had a sizeable immigrant population from East Africa, especially Somali speakers. San Diego had especially been a favorite destination for many of Somali soldiers and their families, given that majority of them had lived in the city while on military training at Camp Pendleton even before the civil war had broken out in Somalia. The weather was great, so no one would be freezing.

## The Second Migration

It was in April of 1995 when we got to San Diego. Some of the family members that we came with to San Diego included my sisters, Nasra (with her husband and children), Fardowsa, Hani, Kowsar and Abdirizak. The rest of my family chose to remain in other areas of Denver or move elsewhere in the US. Wali was one of those who decided to stay in Denver.

We found it easy to settle in the City Heights neighborhood in San Diego, an area with a large immigrant population and a melting pot for cultures from Africa, Asia, Mexico and Latin America. City Heights also boasted of a sizable population of African Americans.

On the down side, in the early 1990's parts of City Heights had a reputation for being high crime areas with prostitution, drugs and gang life. But for refugees escaping from war and miserable life in refugee camps such as Dadaab, City Heights' problems were negligible.

In one of the neighborhoods within City Heights where Somalis had settled, it was said that the police at times did not respond to emergencies as the area was completely under control of gangs. But as the Somali population in the area kept growing between 1992 and 1995, the influence of the gangs on people's lives started decreasing. This happened mainly after the Somalis felt they couldn't escape war at home just to come and live under worse conditions thousands of miles away. As a result, Somali youths who noticed the different ethnic gangs, formed their own outfit, which was known as Rough Tough Somalis (RTS) for 'self-protection'. This of course complicated the safety and security situation, which was already precarious under the activities of so many different gangs.

This gang got involved in frequent fights with indigenous gangs whenever units crossed each others' lines. With time, the local criminal gangs lost control of the area. On their part, Somali community leaders invited the police to take over security matters and a part of the neighborhood was renamed "Bandar-salaam" meaning "land of peace" in Somali language.

In City Heights, we rented two apartments adjacent to each other. Each unit had two bedrooms and baths. What amazed me the most about our apartment buildings was the wide diversity of occupants! Unlike in Denver where we were perhaps the only immigrant community in the entire neighborhood, here we shared a block with Hispanics, Chinese, Cambodians, Vietnamese, Sudanese, and African Americans.

This was where we were to spend our next two years, mostly surviving on welfare and temporary jobs found by my brother Abdirizak and my sister Fardowsa until we found our feet in the area.

In the meantime, many of the misconceptions that I earlier had about life in the United States had come under serious challenge. For instance, while we had always thought that it would be easy to make millions of dollars and send them back to assist our families in Somalia,

Kenya and Ethiopia; here we were once again relying on social support for survival.

Looking back to our work at McDonald's , it was hard to believe that we had to work so hard to earn a meager pay of $4.25 per hour. This was contrary to what we had earlier thought that people in America made tidy sums of money out of menial jobs. Nothing could have been farther from that!

However, a bigger myth that had been busted within the period that I had been in America was that all white people are super rich, they own the latest digital technologies, and they can dish out money left, right and center.

The truth is I had encountered enough white Americans who were penniless and jobless. I knew several of them who also lived on welfare just as we did, and in fact even today they represent the largest welfare recipients. I had now come to appreciate the fact that America is the land of opportunity, but only for those who seize such opportunity.

**Furthering My Education**
In San Diego, I joined Crawford High School in City Heights. One thing I liked about Crawford was that there were many Somali students like me. It was therefore easy to integrate into the school system. With just a little effort, I made new friends with whom we shared more than just culture in common. The downside of it, however, was that I was not learning English as fast as I would have done had I remained in Denver. Later on, I greatly benefited from the International Rescue Committee (IRC) and its after-school program targeting fresh refugees.

My new school did not have as much learning and recreational resources as the more affluent school I had earlier attended in Denver. One of the most frustrating things for me, and I later learned it infuriated other refugee students as well, was  that we were being placed in classes according to our ages as opposed to our skill-set in school.

As such, you could find a seventeen-year-old who had never even held a pen in his or her lifetime placed in tenth grade. Worse still, those who didn't perform well in class were punished for it.

I kept wondering how such a person was expected to compete with students raised in the United States who had had the benefit of starting education from preschool level. This problem of placing students by age as opposed to proficiency is still the case today.

I had by now become a devout basketball player and fan. This is the game that consumed most of my time after school. There were many exciting matches and tournaments, mainly tournaments, organized by the African community in City Heights. There were also tournaments that were organized by the local police department in order to keep youth away from the gangster lifestyle.

In professional basketball, the Chicago Bulls was my favorite team. I had heard of Michael Jordan back in the camps, but to watch him return to the NBA was almost surreal. I liked other Chicago Bulls players too, especially Scottie Pippen for his ingenious moves on the court. I admired their skills in the game and I yearned to play like them.

Although being in the United States had been good so far, the relative sense of insecurity in San Diego often reminded me of how we had survived the bad days in the refugee camps. Denver had been quite peaceful, save for the few times when we discovered our vehicle's tires punctured.

In City Heights I didn't feel safe walking to and from school, especially early mornings and late evenings. There were many sporadic fights between Somalis and indigenous groups who felt threatened by the growing numbers of Somali immigrants in the area.

There were also cultural misunderstandings and differences arising from dress styles, religion and anything else that could create a difference which was unnecessarily exaggerated to the point of causing perpetual tension. The worst street fights were often the ones between Somalis and African Americans.

One would have thought since they have the same origin and color, there would be fewer problems between them. It was argued that African Americans felt that Somalis didn't understand the great sacrifices that African Americans had made so that future generations could live in liberty. As far as the African Americans were concerned, the Somalis seemed to enjoy the freedom with abandon, while they hadn't contributed in any way to its attainment.

Somalis on the other hand felt that African Americans were jealous of Somalis' industriousness, business prowess and ability to rapidly adapt to new environments. To Somalis, African Americans were feeling like a first born kid who wasn't adequately prepared for the coming of another child, thus they just wanted to assert themselves as superior without any justifiable basis other than "we came here before you."

There wasn't any justifiable reason for the street fights; they were a result of myths and stereotyping on both sides.

Given the rising insecurity in the area, my brother Abdirizak and sister Fardowsa often dropped and picked up Hani, Kowsar and me from school. Hani and Kowsar were attending Horace Mann Middle School, which was across from Crawford.

One day, my friend Jamal and I went to play basketball after school at Colina Park, which was a ten minute walk from our apartment. At around 7:00 p.m., we were heading back home when we were accosted by three young Hispanic men.

"Where ya going?" one of the young men shouted.

"That's none of your business," I responded.

"Don't give me attitude you...," the young man responded, sounding quite arrogant.

One of the men walked over to Jamal and stood quite close, as if challenging Jamal's right to stand where he was. "Where did you get that jacket?" he asked Jamal.

Jamal was wearing an expensive San Diego Chargers sports jacket. The Chargers was one of the most popular football teams back then and it had made it to the Super Bowl finals in 1995.

Before Jamal could respond, one of the guys ordered Jamal to take off the jacket and hand it over.

Jamal was not the push over the hill kind, he refused to take it off. He was a tough fighter who had earned himself a number of suspensions from school for being overly defensive and physical.

"Take it off before I knock you down!" was the last order from the tallest of the three rascals, before Jamal's face was covered with a loud slap. I received a blow on the left jaw.

There wasn't time to run or fight back, we were brought down in kicks and blows. Looking up I discovered the gang group had indeed been larger than the initial three who had accosted us. They numbered about seven now.

After they were done with us, we slowly got up and made our way home. Jamal was hospitalized for two weeks for head injuries sustained during the fight.

Here we were, two harmless guys heading home from a game of basketball. We were attacked for the simple reason that we were Somalis and one of us happened to have worn a jacket promoting the team he liked most in football. That is how senseless the cause of the conflicts would sometimes be.

This kind of sporadic fights kept going through out my high school years.

# Part 3

# "Aliens" and the Changing Perceptions

# Chapter 7
# Rediscovering Our Identity
# In Alien Land

Although we had come to the United States as a large family, we were not by any means the first family to undergo the immigration process and we would not be the last. We were just a negligible addition to the ever rising statistics of immigrants to the U.S.

History tells us that America is a land of immigrants who came over seeking better opportunities. This is a quest that sees thousands of people cross the ocean each year. While there are those who come over with nothing, save a strong desire to start life over, again as the case was with my family, there are those who also come over already loaded with great commercial ideas on how they can change America for the better. There is the category that comes over, sees a great business opportunity and runs with it. There are also those who will integrate into this huge economy and make their humble contributions towards a better America one day at a time.

How has America received these adopted children, and to what extent does it recognize their contribution towards the common good of all citizens? Here I will present my opinion, which has been largely shaped by my experiences growing up, learning in schools and from working in the United States I will dig into a little history to illustrate the origins of some of the perceptions that I intend to discuss.

I believe the American immigrant population forms part of the nation's pride and it presents an enormous economic force.

Over half of engineering and technology firm start-ups at Silicon Valley in the period between 1995 and 2005 had one or more immigrants as co-founders. Some of the leading American researchers in nuclear technology, military science, space technology, cancer treatment and virtually any other known field of knowledge are either immigrants or children of immigrants.

How would you account for the thousands of students who come over to the United States for their undergraduate, master's and doctorate studies? Through patenting of inventions and innovations made by such scholars and licensing the commercial exploitation of such knowledge, America maintains its global leadership in research, development and industrial innovation.

I give credit to the United States for creating and maintaining the kind of high-tech institutions that nurture innovations and inventions, as well as channels through which such can be patented and commercialized. Otherwise there would be no huge attraction for scholars across the globe to migrate to the United States and settle down to work.

I know some people would argue that I am applauding the brain drain from the lesser developed world to the global super power. I understand, too, that this is a much more complex debate than can be exhausted in the time

and space I have for this book. However, from my interactions with scholars and innovators who came to work
in the United States, one thing has been common: There
were hardly the kind of opportunities to tap and utilize
the value of their discoveries back at home compared to
what they have found here in the United States. This is
notwithstanding the fact that their knowledge would be
of great benefit to their home economies.

Nonetheless, the majority of them harbor the desire to
one day return home and set up the kind of facilities that
would create opportunities for others seeking to commercialize their ideas. They would wish to someday to
return home more enlightened and able to help set the
systems that would enable their home economies to benefit from the wealth of human intellect in their citizenry.

The same applies to immigrants in other spheres of
life—both large and small players in this economy. I
have been chauffeured around by immigrants who wish
to one day return home and create big businesses.

I was particularly inspired by the dream of Jean Ak-
wasí, a Ghanaian taxi driver in Houston, Texas. The man
in his late thirties told me, as he picked me up from the
airport, that he had saved enough money to enable him
to start a cassava milling business back home.

"That's what I know my people need for now, not an
airport as some politicians keep promising all the time.
The business will help the farmers commercialize what
they grow, and this will put cash directly into their pock-
ets," he said.

This was a young man with a practical idea of how to
solve his people's economic problems, and he was doing

what was required to achieve just that. There are many more immigrants playing silent roles in supporting their economies back home. A look at Diaspora remittances for countries such as China, India, Somalia, South Korea, Nigeria and South Africa, makes one realize that the cash sent from the United States and other western capitals form a significant proportion of those countries' GDP.

I would say having immigrants in the United States is a win-win situation for both the United States and the economies from where the immigrants come from.

The U.S. political leaders often acknowledge the significant role that immigrants have played in making America the great nation it is today. Talking about the need for comprehensive reforms to the American immigration policies in 2011, president Barack Obama (himself a son of an immigrant from Kenya and an American mother) observed that immigrants are not only an integral part of American culture and society, but also important contributors to the U.S. economy. He showed appreciation for the fact that most of the immigrants work and pay taxes, and also create new products, businesses, and technologies that lead to jobs for all Americans.

John Bellows, a key adviser to Tim Geithner, Treasury Secretary, wrote the following in an article titled *The Many Contributions of Immigrants to the American Economy* published in 2011:

*"... While they are only 12 percent of the U.S. population, immigrants represent 16.7 percent of all new business owners in the United States. Immigrants own businesses in a variety of industries and make substantial*

*contributions to both low-skilled and high-skilled sectors: 28.4 percent of businesses owned by those with less than a high school education are owned by immigrants, and 12 percent of businesses owned by those with a college education are owned by immigrants. Overall, immigrants own 10.8 percent of all firms with employees, providing job opportunities for thousands of Americans."*

I believe that these are facts that every immigrant ought to feel proud of, especially coming from the high offices of the government.

Although there are no concise figures on immigrant populations in the United States, data from Pew Hispanic Center, a project of the Pew Research Center, shows that there was a total of 40.4 million immigrants—legal and unauthorized—living in the United States in 2011. This accounted for twelve per cent of the U.S. total population.

The Center for American Progress estimates that it would cost $285 billion over a five-year period to remove all unauthorized immigrants from the United States and to maintain proper border patrols to ensure that foreigners do not return.

On the contrary, the federal government would earn $ 4.5 billion to $5.4 billion in net tax revenues over a period of three years if all undocumented immigrants currently living in the United States were legalized. According to the organization, households headed by unauthorized immigrants paid a total of $11.2 billion in state and local taxes in 2010.

Global statistics show there isn't a jurisdiction in the world that attracts as many immigrants as the United

States. The majority of the immigrants come to the United States in a quest for better economic opportunities and a better quality of education, as well as in escape from war and persecution.

As an immigrant escaping from the war in Somalia, I have taken keen interest in the dynamics of immigration. I have come to appreciate that immigration has been an important pillar for the U.S. cultural and economic progress.

From history, I have learned that the United States has had three major waves of immigration. This began with the colonists in the 1600's, up to 1775, when the Revolutionary War broke out. At that time, the majority of the immigrants were from England, France, Germany, Ireland, Denmark, Ukraine and Sweden, among other nations.

While many of the colonists came to the United States seeking adventure, there were others fleeing from religious persecution. There were convicts from British prisons being dumped here, a faraway country from where they could not escape and return to bother the free and law-abiding citizens.

The second wave of immigration happened between the 1820s and the 1870s, when the economic depression began. The third wave came from 1880s to the early 1920s. The fourth wave, which still continues today, can be traced back to 1965, when the United States amended its immigration laws, reducing restrictions for people seeking to make the United States their second home.

Of all the immigrants coming to the United States in the early days, there was a special kind of people, mainly from Africa. What made them different from other immigrants was  that they were brought here against their will. They were mainly from West Africa, and they were brought here as slaves, to work in white-owned plantations. Out of close to twelve million slaves imported into the Americas in the early 1800s, about 600,000 of them were brought into the United States By 1860 Census, the total slave population in the United States had risen to four million, representing a considerable population of immigrants. Slavery officially ended in 1865 under President Abraham Lincoln.

### Ancient Forms of Prejudice

I would say that the current generation of Americans has perhaps been the most tolerant of all to the presence of immigrants in their midst. I have interacted with Hispanic-Americans, Cuban-Americans, Indian-Americans and African-Americans among others and a common factor cutting across most of them is their gratitude at being called Americans. Although I have been to institutions and forums where racist and derogatory remarks were made against certain sections of the U.S. community, I have found such instances as negligible compared to the hostilities that immigrants went through in the past. I am also aware of the great inequalities that immigrants experience today.

For any immigrant to the United States, nothing can be as comforting as seeing the U.S. Government pursue policies that encourage immigrants to settle here. Through various VISA programs, such as H-1B, H-2A, and H-2B, people from all walks of life have had the lifetime opportunity to come and chase their dreams in a land where it is possible to do so, as opposed to their native homes.

This notwithstanding, the debate continues over the long-term effects of America's continued intake of immigrants, while still outsourcing most of her manufacturing and other business processes to China and other emerging Asian economies. It is such concerns that are leading to agitation for vetting of immigrants to the United States., so that only those with proven professional skills, mainly in the sciences, technology, engineering and mathematics (STEM) disciplines can be allowed entry. This is an ongoing debate and only time will tell how it will end. But a more subtle fact remains that America stands as a global hub of what has come to be known as the knowledge-based economy.

This means that Americans can invent and patent new commercial ideas, but have the industrial production done in countries with more economical costs of production, such as China, India and Thailand. Once the goods are sold, the proceeds come to the U.S. to finance other loops of innovations, and the iteration continues.

I take delight in the fact that liberties have been enhanced for all people coming to America despite the daily challenges faced by people of color.

During the first three immigration waves, often things did not go well for people arriving on American shores from foreign lands. There were constantly open hostilities against the immigrants by the host communities. This is what historians refer to as reaction against strangeness, whereby the natives felt threatened by the "go-getter" character of some immigrant populations.

It is this displeasure with immigrants that led to the false doctrine of racial supremacy. During this historical period, the Anglo-Saxon immigrants were perceived as superior intellectually over the other immigrants.

Seeking better opportunities while running away from the poor economic conditions in their native land, Chinese immigrants set out to work at whatever gave them an earning, no matter how little. This was during the Gold Rush, and many natives felt that the Chinese were being too aggressive in their zest to live; hence, they became objects of ridicule. In 1783, the workforce in the west coast of California began anti-Chinese demonstrations claiming that the Chinese were taking up opportunities meant for the natives. This was to later lead to a law passed that restricted any more immigration of the Chinese to the United States.

There were many forms of segregation too, with Americans of Jewish, Irish and German origin finding it hard to buy properties in high-end districts in the various cities where they settled. It was also not uncommon to find job advertisements made with disclaimers that people of certain descent should not apply. The same was the case in some hotels, too, whereby there were notices that people of certain origin were not welcome.

In 1920, Congress passed yet another landmark law on immigration that locked out Japanese immigrants from setting foot on the U.S. soil. In the meantime, immigrant populations continued facing hostilities and discrimination. This included difficulties in accessing quality education, employment opportunities, and decent housing, even when one had the money to pay for such services.

The same fate befell immigrants from Mexico. Mexican-Americans rarely had the kind of life they had hoped for coming to America. Their children were often denied access to education and employment opportunities.

The immigrant population in the United States continued to grow, especially through birth. There was intensive agitation for equal liberties for all Americans, their descent notwithstanding. This led to important changes in legislation, which eventually created greater equality among all Americans.

Levels of tolerance among the various communities across the United States have been on the increase, and respect for the civil liberties for all has since been on an upward trajectory. It is no wonder that most American organizations today take pride in using the phrase "we are an equal opportunity employer." This means that one's racial, religious, gender or other affiliations notwithstanding, what matters most to the American economy is one's ability to deliver on the action points outlined in the employment contract.

The struggle to adapt to a new way of life is perhaps one of the greatest challenges that immigrants face. Though some possess Basic English communication skills, the struggle to make a decent living day-by-day takes up much of the time that the immigrants would have otherwise spent learning a profession that could uplift their quality of life. This has been one of my foremost concerns since I got here.

I have particularly observed this among the Somali community in Minneapolis and elsewhere in the United States Of all immigrant communities in the United

States, Somalis, one of the most recent arrivals, face arduous challenges in integrating into the mainstream American life. In addition to the barriers faced by all immigrants and refugees, Somalis face specific structural barriers due to unfair association with violence, piracy and terrorism.

I still recall life at Crawford's High school and how challenging it was to integrate with other communities. I remember that at one point students from other communities would get frowned at for harboring the idea of befriending a Somali student. Although we tried to remain composed in the face of the many misconceptions about our way of life, sporadic street fights with Hispanic and African-American gangs served to paint the Somali community as being equally abrasive.

As a product of both the Somali culture and the American culture, some key differences stand out for me. For instance, one aspect of Somali lifestyle that has for long been misunderstood is religion. Most Somalis profess Islam, which requires women to dress in clothes that cover their bodies from head to toe. This is unlike the western lifestyle, which doesn't bear restrictions on one's dressing. In some places and occasions for instance, the lesser covered a woman's body is, the more she is regarded as socially fitting in.

Muslim women are discouraged from shaking hands with men, save for the women's husbands, brothers, fathers and nephews. To most people in mainstream America, this failure to receive an outstretched hand in greeting has often been viewed as snobbish. However, the Somali women are doing nothing more than maintaining religious purity. Despite the cultural and religious requirements, I have noticed nowadays that the majority of Somali women shake hands with male counterparts.

The Somali culture discourages the girls from dating people from other communities. However, this is not special to Somalis, it happens in many cultures.

Parties that involve consumption of alcohol form part of the mainstream American life. This is especially common in college campuses over the weekends, during graduations, at weddings and other social events that bring people together. Consumption of alcohol is forbidden in Islam.

This means that there are fewer opportunities for interactions between Somali young men and women and people from other communities, which hinders the extent to which other communities could socialize and get to understand why the Somalis behave the way they do.

For this reason, I opine that much of the discrimination that people of Somali origin face in the United States has mainly been based on lack of understanding, as well as on common stereotypes of characters of wayward individuals being ascribed to the entire community.

For instance, I remember an incident at JBS Swift & Co., a Nebraska-based meat processing facility, which caught the nation's attention for the wrong reasons. The year was 2007. The firm had lost quite a sizeable workforce, most of them 'illegal' immigrants from Latin America, who had been arrested in readiness for deportation. The company's quest for affordable labor saw them hire a total of 400 Somali immigrants from the Somali community in Nebraska.

It did not take long before tensions started brewing between the Somalis and other workers as a result of the Somali's observation of religious obligations. As Muslims, the Somalis had to take breaks for prayers as required by their religion. But to the rest of the workforce and the management, the Somalis were heaving the burden of meeting production targets on the non-Muslims, who had to be left working while the Somalis took their prayer breaks.

As a result, some of the Somalis lost their jobs for taking unofficial breaks, which according to the management, were hurting the company's productivity. Other immigrant communities working at the firm, among them Sudanese, who didn't practice Islam, retained their jobs, as they hadn't taken any additional breaks to pray.

Although the fired Somalis engaged a lawyer to argue for their case in court on the basis of religious discrimination, this left other employers wary of hiring Somalis. The few Somalis who remained at the meat facility were left in a Catch-22 situation, whereby they had to choose between their religion and keeping the job.

## Disabusing Piracy and Terrorism

Although there is no single and universally accepted explanation of the origin of piracy on the coast of Somalia, there are many documented incidents of the vice. One such account was written as far back as 150 AD by Claudius Ptolemy, in Geographia. What is beyond doubt; however, is that the fall of the Somali government in 1991 meant that there was no authority with a legal mandate to administrate over the country's territorial waters.

With fishing as a key economic activity along the Somalia coast, allegations started emerging that some
international sea liners were dumping toxic waste on
Somalia's waters, which had the effect of polluting the
ocean, killing the fish, and thus hurting the people's livelihood, according to the UN Environment Programme
(UNEP).

This seemed to "legitimize" attacks by armed groups
on foreign ships passing through Somalia's territorial
waters within the Indian Ocean and by making foreign
ships pay a fine for the pollution. This grew into a worse
problem, whereby the pirates started attacking ships
sailing in international waters and through the Gulf of
Aden and demanding a ransom for their release and the
release of the ships' crews.

One of the most daring piracy activities carried out by
Somalis on Indian Ocean waters was the capture of MV
Faina. This was on September 25, 2008. While this was by
no means the first ever ship to be hijacked, it was the nature of its cargo that made this case particularly of international significance. The cargo included 33 T-72 tanks
from Ukraine, as well as rocket-propelled grenades and
ammunition. The ship was bound for the port of Mombasa in Kenya.

While the pirates claimed that they were not privy to
the cargo until the ship was captured, they went  ahead
to demand $35 million as ransom for the ship's release.
But this was not the only twist in the story.

Word had it that the cargo belonged to the Government of Southern Sudan, yet there was an arms embargo
imposed on South Sudan by the UN, thanks to the dec-

ades of war with the North. This happened before the separation of the two to form independent states in July 2011.

With the arms embargo in force, it meant that South Sudan rebels could not legally purchase weapons from the international market. Likewise, selling such weapons, or aiding the region to access weapons was a violation of the embargo that would lead to sanctions.

There was international scare of the impact of such weaponry falling into the hands of Somali pirates and possibly terrorist groups. For this reason, the U.S. Navy, among other navies patrolling the Indian Ocean waters, surrounded the ship to prevent any offloading of the cargo by the pirates.

Five months later on February 4, 2009, MV Faina was released after its owners parted with over $3million in ransom.

Thereafter, the Government of Kenya insisted that the weaponry onboard MV Faina had been purchased for use by the Kenya Defense Forces. However, there are credible reports including satellite images showing the cargo being offloaded in Kenya, and being mounted on rail tracks and transported to South Sudan.

The matter of pirates attacking ships in international waters had threatened to blow the lid off sensitive matters of defense procurements by the Government of Southern Sudan. In the process, this complicated matters for Kenya, a neighbor to both Somalia and Southern Sudan, especially regarding Kenya's purported assistance to transit arms and military equipment through its soil to a jurisdiction already under a UN arms embargo. The matter eventually fizzled out.

Although piracy might have been a big problem to the international community, what most people did not know is that it was indeed a double-edged sword, cutting and wounding in equal measures the international community as well as the local innocent Somali population.

Previously, the absence of a national government meant that imports such as sugar, rice, corn meal, clothes and shoes, among others, could be smuggled with ease into Somalia via the port of Kismayu as well as in other ports. This meant easy access to the basics of food and clothing as most of the imports didn't attract tax, save for the "facilitation fees" paid out to illegal forces manning the port and transport corridors.

With the advent of piracy, the cost of essential goods went through the roof, since no one dared conduct business with Somalia for fear of abduction and exorbitant ransom cash that the pirates would demand. The hijacking menace became so rampant that gun men would take over vessels carrying humanitarian assistance meant for fellow Somalis and demand ransom for release of the vessels.

In October 2005, a vessel registered as MV Miltzow owned by Motaku Shipping Agencies based in Mombasa, Kenya, was hijacked with 850 tons of food aid destined for Somalia. The cargo belonged to the United Nations' World Food Programme (WFP). In June of the same year, another vessel, MV Semlow, also chartered by WFP, had been hijacked off Somalia coast, ferrying 850 tons of rice for an estimated 28,000 survivors of the tsunami in Somalia's Puntland region. Though the vessels were later released, the incidents had served as a good illustration of some Somalis biting the very hand that fed them. This only served to scare off any would-be trader dreaming of doing business with Somalia.

With the increased cases of ransom money running into hundreds of millions of dollars paid to the pirates, this brought about a different kind of problem to Somalis—inflation. Now that there were few if any imports of food and other essential supplies coming into Somalia, it meant that the millions of dollars paid as ransom to pirates only came to chase away the scarce supplies already in the market. Therefore, the commodities were sold to the highest bidder, meaning that ordinary folks could hardly afford the basics of food, clothing and shelter.

The cost of doing business on the East African coast, including cost of essential goods such as oil imported from the Middle East going through the Gulf of Aden, shot higher than anyone would have hoped for. The cost of insurance for vessels plying the East African routes also increased dramatically. The World Bank estimated that Somali piracy was driving up the cost of global trade by $18 billion annually. The majority of Somalis, both at home and in the Diaspora, were calling on the international community to step in and help end the piracy by helping Somalis establish an effective central government.

The piracy problem has since been brought under control. This was mainly after the UN Security Council passed several resolutions in 2008, among them one proposed by Britain, introducing tougher sanctions against Somalia over the country's failure to prevent a surge in sea piracy. This opened up an opportunity for NATO countries, the United States, Russia, India and China to move in with naval vessels to curb the problem.

With increased international military activity against piracy, the rate of successful capture of ships was reduced from fifty-three vessels in 2010, to only one by the third quarter of 2012. In essence, this closed the era of sea terrorism. However, many Somali-Americans often find themselves in the awkward position of having to explain to other Americans that piracy was a criminal activity benefiting only a few individuals, not all Somalis.

It was simply a bad situation whereby a few powerful individuals were holding the entire nation of Somalia at ransom, profiteering from inconveniences caused to global trade, and using force to silence the ordinary Somalis who dared raise a finger at the crimes being committed in the high seas. Truth is, the majority of Somali-Americans have indeed never even seen a pirate. They read and watch stories about the menace on local and international media like everyone else, but come to bear the brunt of a negative image over issues they have absolutely no control over.

Ultimately, there have been suggestions made on how to ensure that the blow dealt to piracy on Somali waters by the combined international forces is final. Some people have advocated for the formation of a Somali Coast Guard to police the country's territorial waters. Others have spoken in favor of building further the capacity of the Kenyan naval force, Somalia's neighbor to the south, and increase its mandate to cover Somali's territorial waters, especially given the amount of resources that would be required to create a Somali command from scratch.

I know some of these approaches have been advanced with Somali's interests at heart. However, I agree with the school of thought that seeks to prioritize institution-building across Somalia in line with the country's new constitution.

As per the new constitution, there is need to recognize among other things, the diversity and aspirations of Somali communities; hence, the call for a federal state with distinct federal governments at the grassroots. In my opinion, such a system of governance will present Somali people with an opportunity to set their own priorities—including security matters—at the grassroots levels, and have a national government articulating the collective vision of the people.

Another stereotypical representation of Somalis has been in association with the al-shabaab. Also known as Harakat al-Shabaab al-Mujahideen (HSM), the Somalia-based outfit has been branded as a terror network by the Somali people, regional governments, the United States, and by the international community in general.

Al-shabaab is an off-shoot of the Islamic Courts Union, which controlled Mogadishu and much of Southern Somalia till they were driven out by the Transitional Federal Government (TFG) and Ethiopian forces in 2006.

Ideologically, the outfit has been waging war against what it perceives as enemies of Islam, including other Muslims who don't' subscribe to their ideology, as well as the western nations and their interests in Somalia and the greater East African region. Al Shabaab set out to institute a strict and radical interpretation of their version of Islam.

The terror network has for long been believed to have links with al-Qaeda, and some of its top leadership is believed to have been behind the twin bombing of the U.S. Embassies in Nairobi and Dar-es-Salaam in 1998, as well as a string of violent attacks on recreational facilities in Somalia, Kenya and Uganda.

Unbeknown to most people is the fact that al-Shabaab has wrecked more havoc on Somali people than on anyone else in the world. If you have ever heard of barbaric terrorism, then that is al-Shabaab for you. Think of a network that amputates a seven-year-olds hand allegedly for "stealing" a loaf of bread to tame hunger pangs. This is the same network that would maim a poor widow for the crime of failing to part with "protection" fee, while in reality she has no cash left to even feed her six children.

Somalia is littered with thousands of graves of many whose torture and unceremonious deaths in the hands of al-Shabaab remain unexplained. There are many more Somalis going about their businesses in the shame and disgust of having had their limbs amputated in public squares in full glare of the masses as al-Shabaab's strict punishment for the victims' misdemeanors.

The terror network had bestowed upon itself the sacred duty of redefining Somalia, by first changing the people's national symbols. To al-Shabaab, the Somali's national blue flag has failed the people, and only a black one can inspire people's hopes and aspirations and light the nation's dreams of prosperity once more.

Furthermore, the network had redefined Somalism as a global ideology shared by all who have a belief system and a soul as virtuous as that of al-Shabaab. This meant that Somalia was open to people of all walks of life from across the globe, provided they shared a common vision of maiming, beheading and stoning to death those who went against the ideals of the terror network. To achieve this, the network was intent on abolishing the Somalia national language!

To the terror network, ordinary Somalis had failed by observing peaceful Islam, and this had been the cause of the conflicts that had now befallen the nation. To tame the problem, al-Shabaab had prescribed a false interpretation of Islam.

A more shocking revelation of the extent of the terror network's ability to recruit came with the disappearance of youth of Somali-American descent from the state of Minnesota. It was later discovered that the youths had travelled back to Somalia to take part in al-Shabaab's terror activities. While some of the youths volunteered their media skills to make propaganda videotapes for use by the terror group, a good number of the Somali-Americans ended up dying in armed conflicts between al-Shabaab and the Somali government forces and the African peacekeepers under the African Mission in Somalia (AMISOM).

It was alleged that al-Shabaab was drawing financial support from its sympathizers in the United States. To curb this, U.S. banks halted all forms of financial transfers to Somalia. The effects of this were disastrous to the ordinary Somali people wishing to send financial assistance to Somalia.

While al-Shabaab sympathizers could find alternative means of sending the cash to support the movement's criminal activities, it was now impossible for Somali-Americans working as taxi drivers and dish washers among other low paying jobs, to send money for food, shelter and school fees to their children back in Somalia. It also became increasingly difficult to send home financial assistance for the ill, as well as for the elderly, who could not eke out a living in the war-torn country.

Although al-Shabaab is still perceived as a threat, it was routed from its last bastion in Kismayu in southern Somalia by combined efforts of the local Somali forces, Federal government forces and the Kenya Defense Forces working under AMISOM. But with the effects of September 11 still fresh on people's minds, the sight of Muslims clad in hijabs reminds many mainstream Americans of their vulnerability from within their own territory. As such, Muslims are often treated with caution and suspicion. Somali-Americans being the most visible face of Islam in the communities where they live, the same blanket and stereotypical treatment have been extended to them by default.

As a Somali-American professing Islam who is a student of Western thought, this at times makes me feel like a prisoner of conscience. The constitution grants me and everyone else in this great land inalienable rights and liberties. One of them is freedom of association. But how effectively can one exercise this when some of the members of the society where they live treat them with suspicion?

While there are delinquents in virtually every community on earth (and that is why criminal justice systems exist) it would be in order to treat each member of the

American community on the basis of the individual's character. If a white American gets drunk and pees by the road side, as intelligent people, we don't need anyone to explain to us that that this was a misdemeanor by a single individual, and not the entire community in which that individual belongs. Now you understand why it is unintelligent to generalize this matter and assert that all white Americans get drunk and pee by the roadside?

Likewise, if a member of the Somali community in the United States engages in a misdemeanor or crime, we need to isolate that particular case as it involves the individual, and not indict the entire community. Similarly, if a radicalized Muslim youth joins a terror network, it would be good to remember that not all Muslims are radical, and not all have joined, or ever dream of joining any radical groups. The majority of Somali-Americans, while practicing Islamic faith, might not know a thing about radicalization. They are just like you and me, busy working to make ends meet. They have bills they must pay, children to educate, mortgages to finance, and above all, dreams in life that they strive to achieve every day.

I believe the American dream is achievable by all. I have met many enterprising Somalis who own some of the largest businesses in their cities. I meet many Somali-Americans who have gone to school here and are lawyers, doctors, engineers and scholars in some of the leading American universities. This shows that the American dream is possible, but only for those who are brave enough to challenge their circumstances, rise above prejudice and misperceptions and fight on towards their destiny. This is the case whether you are Somali, Mexican, Chinese, Japanese, or any other prefix you might place before your American identity.

One of the things we remind ourselves as new Americans is that one doesn't  have to abandon his/her identity, culture or lifestyle to be accepted as an American. Integrating into the American society is not the same thing as assimilation.

As the "salad bowl" theory of American integration suggests, America is a multi-cultural society. The various communities come together with their distinct cultures, traditions and lifestyles—much like salad ingredients— and this is what gives the U.S. its freshness and flavor.

As sociologists will tell you, though cultures may differ in their outlook of things, there isn't a single culture in the world that is superior to others. As such, you can remain who you are and be recognized as an American.

# Part 4

# Shaping the Future

# Chapter 8
## Quest for Education

After the tribulations that we went through as a family to escape the war in Somalia, finding our way to the United States seemed like the single pill that would heal all the wounds in our lives. I felt that I had gotten the most important solution to our life's miseries and as if we could just push the doors and lock out what had so far been the worst chapter of our lives. Or was it escapism—literally speaking? Like most immigrants, I had all along developed the notion that upon getting to the United States I would quickly enroll in a good school, earn my degree and enter the job market and the rest would be history.

By God's grace I made it to America with my family, but only to discover that it takes effort and decisiveness to succeed. Nothing comes easy and luck is a rare commodity here. It's all about seizing the moment and making the best use of available opportunities. I learned too that opportunities don't come labeled as such, but they pass by disguised as ugly years of hard work and self-sacrifice and confronting many challenges.

I also came to realize that like everywhere else, it's hard to advance in the States without a long-term vision of what you want in life. Short sightedness is the easiest route to the rat-race kind of life, where you only make what you need to survive through a given day. I came to understand the sad fact that despite being born, brought up, educated and now living in one of the most advanced economies, the average American lives on credit card and rarely saves.

It is this state of affairs that ensnares most new immigrants to the United States, limiting their ability to pursue their lifetime dreams, and thus they end up choosing the easiest way out of the highway to success.

Looking back, I realize that getting an education was the best decision I ever made and at the right moment in my life for that.

I thank God too, that I had the support from my family to keep me going, never mind that on many occasions there would be no leisure at home owing to my school expenses. We had to choose the not-so-flashy clothing, and we also had to moderate on what we ate too, among other austerity measures.

As I write this book, I work as a Program Officer for Margaret A. Cargill Philanthropies (MACP), one of the largest philanthropies in the United States managing grants worth millions of dollars. All this makes me feel that to a large extent, the sacrifices that my family made to see me through school definitely paid off.

I might never be able to afford to repay every one of them for the sacrifices they made for me. In my community, paying off your parents or elders for bringing you up or for the sacrifices they made for you is a taboo— we leave that to God, as there isn't any possible way to pay them back individually. But making sacrifices to help someone get through a certain course in life is not in vain.

The person you are helping out might never be able to repay you for your sacrifices, but nothing can be as gratifying as seeing the person find his own feet and grow into an independent person, capable of going about his or her life and assisting others. This brings to mind the old Chinese saying: "If you are planning for a year, sow rice; if you are planning for a decade, plant trees; if you are planning for a lifetime, educate people."

Prior to joining the MACP, I served as a Senior Program Officer at Alliance Healthcare Foundation, a San Diego-based organization working to improve access to healthcare in underserved communities. In this capacity, I managed community grants totaling more than $25 million annually. This was out of the understanding that some human needs, such as healthcare, are universal and are a necessity whether one can afford them or not.

From 2001 to 2008, I was the Associate Executive Director for Horn of Africa, an anchor refugee assistance and nonprofit organization based in San Diego. Horn of Africa provides cultural and linguistic services to refugees and immigrants and helps them settle down and begin life in the U.S. In 2008, I helped to establish the Institute for Horn of Africa Studies and Affairs, (IHASA) which is now one of the leading grass-root think-tanks about the Horn of Africa region and in the diaspora.

With particular focus on the Horn of Africa region, IHASA employs a three-pronged implementation strategy to achieve comprehensive regional peace, security and economic integration in the following sequences:

## Peace Building

With the region being one of the most afflicted by armed conflicts and crime arising from proliferation of small arms crossing borders into otherwise peaceful states from the war-torn areas, IHASA holds that the basis for achieving a peaceful and integrated Horn of Africa (HOA) region primarily hinges first on mapping conflicts, followed by building the architecture or constituents for peace.

## Good Governance

The second element in implementing the organization's long-term vision is to promote good governance and an inclusive democratic system. This comes from the belief that people follow rules that they participate in formulating and that legitimacy to lead must come from the people being led. Promotion of democracy in the region is thus a key pillar of IHASA.

## Economic Integration

The ultimate hope for the Horn of Africa region to enhance its economic and social development lies in the integration of its various economies. This is because the people need trading opportunities and trading partners. The countries in the region present the best opportunities for intra-regional trade. However, this can only be achieved after peace and good governance have been instituted.

My current roles are light-years away from the Hamse Warfa who once washed dishes at a McDonald's Center at Denver in order to place a meal on his table. Had you told me back then—when I hardly had a nickel to my name—that I would at one time be managing funds worth millions of dollars annually, and that I would at one time in my life be influencing important public policies, I would have perhaps called you a dreamer. But through God's grace, I have done that and much more all in a span of less than nineteen years since coming here as a refugee from Africa, armed with the barest of basic language skills.

By saying this, I don't wish to imply that my current position is the highest position that a Somali immigrant has ever attained in the U.S. I don't wish to imply, too, that any of my current or past positions should be the standard by which Somali or any other immigrants should gauge their success or that I have reached the zenith. Far from that, I appreciate that there are many ladders to success in one's line of calling, and I only use these examples to gauge my personal advancement towards my destiny in life.

I wish to salute all immigrants who have had to overcome worse odds both at home and in foreign countries to accomplish even greater feats in the United States or elsewhere. Pausing to look back and to scrutinize the circumstances under which I have been operating, coming this far feels like a great milestone, though the road ahead is still long.

Perhaps the most important determinant in my progress through life has been education. I will forever remain grateful for the insight that God gave to my family who insisted I must remain in school even during tough economic times, when I didn't understand their obsession with having me get an education.

While in Somalia, Dad had made quite a handsome investment in our education. He had ensured that we attended good schools and that my elder brothers and sisters enrolled in good universities. We were always encouraged to emulate our elder siblings, with emphasis being laid on education as the key to better life.

True as this might have been back then, I think it has been made more vivid by our immigration to a land miles away from home, where in my opinion, education is the most effective way of making a head start and fusing into the new culture and lifestyle for a new immigrant like I once was. I have met many Somalis who held prominent positions back home, but who had to make do with menial jobs upon coming to America for the simple reason that though privileged to come here, they had little education, or that their educational papers were not recognized here.

Unfortunately, unless such people take up professionally recognized courses in the United States or start businesses and run them successfully, they might remain disadvantaged and in poverty in a world where the cost of living keeps escalating.

This predicament faces many immigrants from across the world. There will be children of high ranking government and business executives who take refuge in Western countries once there is trouble back home, only to resort to humiliating lifestyles for lack of proper education, or for lack of recognition of their educational qualifications.

I still recall my part time work at a McDonald's outlet in Denver. It felt like a privilege to get such an opportunity, given my family's dire financial situation upon immigrating to the U.S. I did the job with my two brothers. It was a tough beginning to life but what options did my brothers and I have? We had to work hard to earn a pittance, and I can't tell just how much I hated that kind of lifestyle. I always told myself that if there was anything I could do to get myself out of that kind of job I would surely do it without ever turning back.

## Striving for Dad's Dream

My quest for education was driven by many factors and it was a fight against many odds. I had to live true to my late father's vision for me and my brothers and sisters— he had always wanted his children to get the best of education and live a good life. In order to keep my dad's memories alive, I had to attend school and to work hard.

I wanted to make significant contributions to people's lives—to mobilize support to empower people who had, like my family and I, fallen victim to circumstances beyond their understanding and control. The only way I could figure out how to achieve this was by interaction with people of influence. If I were to interact with them at an equal level so as to get assistance without feeling like a beggar, I had to rise to their levels. The only way to do this was through a good education, so I could better articulate the issues of the people in need.

Our family settled in San Diego after leaving Denver. This felt much more like home, especially given the large community of Somali immigrants in the neighborhood. My thirst for education drove me to seek admission at Crawford High School. Eager as I was to learn, I had to first enroll for English classes so as to improve my language proficiency. This was the only way I could manage my academic pursuits since every academic discipline was taught and tested in English. After all, English was the medium of communication in school and in almost every other sphere of the American life.

From my earlier school interactions in Denver, I had learned a little bit of English, but most were words picked up from playing basketball.

As it often happens, age mates devise their language and symbols, which they adopt as their de-facto mode of communication within their interaction circles. Some common English words were used denotatively or referenced completely out of context in order to create a weird kind of language that only we understood.

My peers had also perfected the art of using obscene words and expressions veiled as an important part of everyday communication. As someone learning English as a second language, I on various occasions found myself innocently bringing the obscenities from the basketball court to the classroom, much to the dismay of my teachers and fellow students.

Consequently, I got reprimanded by one of my teachers. As a result, I became dejected and abstained from formal discussions in class and outside the classroom, as I was no longer sure of the meaning of what would come out of my mouth.

Schooling with a large population of Somalis in San Diego didn't help the situation. Although our teachers did their best in helping us learn English, we often found ourselves conversing in our native language, as soon as the teacher left the classroom. We would then dash out for break shouting in Af-Soomaali, Somali's national language.

Part of this came from the usual nature of teenage rebellion, sometimes against the very course that is meant to help them. But rebellion is not an academic discipline: nowhere was anyone going to sit for a test in rebellion. Little did we know that we were not helping ourselves in mastering the new language on which our survival, integration and growth in America was hinged on. Like many Somalis in my group of friends, I kept posting poor academic grades. This was compounded by poor performance in class and it broke my spirit in the fight for my educational goals.

Although I used to read much and could understand almost every concept that the teacher taught in class, I came to discover later that poor language skills meant that I couldn't express myself adequately to demonstrate my understanding. By extension, I am not sure I could have passed most exams even if they had been administered orally.

It's for this reason that I started regretting not having taken the free English language classes that had been offered at the refugee camps back in Kenya. Although these were not professionally graded lessons, but rather informal teachings, those of us who had taken the classes seriously were coping much better with academic work and social life in America.

This made me feel as though I had missed an important part of camp life, having chosen soccer rather than education. This is a case of poor decision-making based on lack of foresight! But I believe I was just a kid with no foresight of what was before me, rather I was more inclined towards passion than towards purpose. Nevertheless, living as a refugee was the lowest part of my life because being in such a situation hope seemed like delusion.

With the challenges I was finding in learning English, I had come to appreciate just how much foresight the camp administrators had to have had to start language and basic education classes at the camp, and just how ignorant I must have been to dismiss the classes.

During my lowest moments while at Crawford's High School, I would find solace and acceptance in the basketball court, where my contribution was gaining significant acknowledgement from my peers. I was taller than many players and this gave me an added advantage in the game, to the extent that everyone wanted me on their team.

It was this quest for a sense of meaning that got the better part of me. It became an escape from the reality that I was not performing as I should have been doing in class. Each time we did continuous assessment tests and I was among those with poor performances, I would long for the break time so that I could reassure myself that I was worth something in the field.

The idea of escaping to the field every time I felt inadequate in class became an obsession and that eventually led me into other regrettable decisions. The greatest among them was that I chose sports over academic work. I unfortunately ended up with a badly dislocated left ankle in the basketball court.

This meant that I was to keep away from the field on the doctor's advice so as to allow the ankle to heal. On the contrary, the obsession to play got the better part of me and I was once again on the field, with the injured ankle barely recovered enough to sustain the strain of the game.

As a result, I toppled over after a hard hit by an opponent during a game. Deep within I could feel a buildup of pain that was just waiting to erupt. I hurried to the school's clinic for assistance. The long and short of it was that the injury got worse and it took almost a year to heal.

## Redefining Myself

The idea of keeping away from basketball somehow brought much-needed balance in my life. I was off the court for some time and I couldn't bear just going there to see my friends play without me getting to touch the ball. I somehow found myself avoiding the field and going back to the core business of education.

I missed out on the game but this gave me rare moments of reflections on who I was and the circumstances under which I was now living. It is then that I started asking myself hard questions, the most important one being what I really wanted to do and achieve in life. I was beginning to get fed up with playing catch-up on everything that mattered.

Mom and my elder brothers and sisters took notice of the changes taking place in me and they began nudging me to work harder on my education and to move away from sports and partying. I was not particularly a party animal, but their interest was to get me focused on the difficult path to success.

Mom became more sensitive towards my feelings. She became inquisitive of my experiences in school, what we had learned and whether I needed any special assistance. We began speaking English in most of our conversations at home—if only to provide my sisters and me with an environment to practice the language without criticism. Wali offered to hire a tutor for me but it never got to that; I was beginning to show great improvement on my academic record. Finally I realized that I was on the right track to academic success, thanks in part to my injured ankle. I enrolled in the International Rescue Committee's afterschool ESL program, which was instrumental in helping me improve my English competence.

As a young immigrant to the United Stats, my idea of fun had consisted of watching sports, playing basketball, running, going to the beach every weekend, and watching movies. But I had been sort of an odd duck when it came to adopting the mainstream American culture. I did not embrace many things such as drinking alcohol, listening rap music, eating large amounts of food or celebrating Halloween and Valentines' Day. I abstained from these activities and many others as a matter of choice but also in consideration of my culture. While there are many things that define us as Americans, our diversity is what makes America a prodigious nation. I celebrate the Fourth of July, Memorial Day, and all other national holidays.

Gradually, I redefined my personality and discovered better things that I could do with my time, especially now that I was focusing less on basketball. In addition, I realized that there was need for better understanding of the African community at Crawford High School in order to better articulate our unique needs. Therefore, I helped establish the African Student Union in the school. This brought together students of African descent in the school and it gave us a common identity and a platform from which to communicate.

This also made me realize that I had leadership traits. My teachers lauded me for the initiative, and they often referred to the association as a good example of a vehicle of positive influence.

Under the association, we held numerous discussions on how African immigrants could integrate into American life but at the same time remain true to their identity. We engaged constructively on the role that Africans in foreign countries could play to help bring better governance and development to their respective countries of origin and the African continent at large. We occasionally invited teachers and other resourceful persons from outside the school to come talk to us on various issues such as achieving academic success, and making career choices.

Engagement in these discourses helped us foster stronger bonds of unity and enabled us to understand ourselves better, stand with each other in times of need, and keep off from negative thoughts and deeds as teenagers.

The more I engaged in such constructive activities, the more I felt a buildup of positive energy within me. I was developing a strong sense of purpose in what I was doing, an awakening, of sorts, to the reality that there was a lot hidden within me that I needed to exploit.

I felt the urge to discover myself more. I felt inclined to want to know what else I could do and how. I was beginning to see more sense in life—a shedding off of the earlier feel of hopelessness with which I had traversed Somalia's jungles looking for hope.

I felt that, if there was anything I could do to make my life more sensible, I was ready for it. If that meant mastering the English language, then I was up to the challenge. With the positive responses that I was getting in class for improved performance, and in the wider school community for being a founding member of the association that brought together students of African-American immigrants, I certainly felt motivated to work harder in my education.

From the several career talks that we had been given in school, I decided to set high targets for myself and work towards their achievement. After all, what couldn't I become in life if I had self-belief and determination?

Thus, I decided that I would become a pharmacist. I put all my efforts at studies so as to meet the required qualifications for admission into a bachelor's degree in pharmacy.

My dream was to set up a chain of drug stores across the United States and in developing countries and spend the proceeds in making life better for my fellow human beings, especially refugees and the people we had left behind in the camps in Kenya, Ethiopia and Somalia. Though thousands of miles away, I always feel solidarity for the poor people we left behind.

Thoughts of how I can pull my people out from their deplorable living conditions and give them dignified sources of livelihood pre-occupy my mind now as they did back then. If it was within my power to make just one wish come true, it would be to see lasting peace restored in the world, especially Somalia, so that her children can return home from across the world, and start rebuilding their country.

However, upon graduating from high school my grades did not meet the threshold for admission into a good school of pharmacy. This was a major setback to my dream career. I felt as though I could return to school and retake the exam. But then a new reality dawned on me. It had been a financial struggle to go through high school. My family could not afford to pay for my degree in pharmacy at the university even if I posted great results in high school and government financial aid might be sufficient.

Of course this was the only way to rationalize my not-so-good scores, given that perhaps I could have gotten scholarships to complete my studies if I done well. At times I think I was limiting the extent to which God's providence would have played a role in making my dream career come true. I focused more on the problem than the solution—I just wasn't sure that I could have gotten the kind of money that was required to see me through the course in college.

On second thought, I felt that maybe God had a different plan for my life—this is perhaps why God hadn't allowed me to attain the grades required for pharmaceutical training. Instead, I opted for an associate degree in

Computer Information Systems and a certificate in Microcomputer professionals at San Diego City College.

Although I could have easily gone straight to San Diego State University, I chose to go to the community college first so as to first secure an Associate Degree. My reasoning was that due to the unpredictability of life that could easily complicate my completion of a four-to-five-year degree course, it would have been much safer to first secure a two-year Associate Degree and proceed to the full degree, at a later date. Much of this concern of unpredictability relates to the unpredictable way in which my family and I have lived so far.

Being armed with an associate degree would have allowed me the chance of getting a good job and earning enough cash to pay my way through whatever level of education I fancied. Hence, in 1998 I enrolled at San Diego City College. I graduated in 2000 with the Associate Degree. I also completed all transfer courses needed to pursue the full degree program at San Diego State University. In addition, I completed a microcomputer professional certificate at San Diego City College.

**Higher Education**

With the Associate Degree safely in my pocket, I felt that I could pause and work for some time and then go back to college a few years later. What's more, I had already secured what I considered a well-paying job, although it was a temporary one.

With my newly found economic freedom, I wanted to contribute financially to my family's upkeep, considering the difficulties they had gone through to educate me. The foremost thought on my mind was to help my mother start a business, which would make her financially independent.

I recalled our earlier days in Mogadishu, where she had run a successful clothing store in the city. Her age notwithstanding, she was an expert in women's fashion. She still had the connections in Italy and China that she could use to import designer wear into the States, and this was a line of business I was willing to help her restart. I figured that with some savings, especially now that I was working, I could take up a loan with my job as the security and set her off to success in business.

However great and irresistible the idea appeared to me, my family did not vouch for it. Wali argued that though having Mom return to business was a good idea, the circumstances had changed. We were no longer in Mogadishu where almost everyone knew mom, so it would take considerable amounts of time and ridiculous amounts of resources to set up and advertise the clothes business. This was not discounting the fact that purchasing and bringing in stock from Italy and China would also require a tidy sum of money.

To my surprise, Wali argued that the person in whom the family should invest a fraction of the amount I had in mind and bring better returns for us all was me.

"You are younger and much more energetic than Mom. We have not yet gotten tired of paying for your school expenses, and we are doing this for your best interest. When you achieve success in life, you can come back and do whatever favor you wish for anyone of us, Mom included. We will all be grateful. But for now, we need your future secured through education. That was dad's dream," he said.

I had not looked at it this way. I hadn't visualized my education as a family investment. Actually I had never paused to wonder why everyone had worked so hard to make sure I had everything I needed to see me through school. For the first time, I recognized that education is a good long-term investment—just like real estate—with expected tangible returns. This revelation was simply overwhelming.

Although I didn't fancy going back to class, my fate was sealed. As an African saying goes, an elder who is sitting down can see farther than a boy perched on top of a tall tree. Here, I was the boy on top of the tree and I had to come down and heed to my elders' wisdom. I succumbed to the pressure and enrolled at San Diego State University for a bachelor's degree in Political Science.

I thought that my family was overbearing and that they were intruding onto my life, but today I appreciate that they were right and I was wrong. They were truly sent by God to show me the path and purpose that He had for my life. Had I taken a break from school, perhaps I would never have gone back! The temptations of a well-paying job and a lifestyle devoid of tedious academic assignments would have consumed the zeal I had for a better world.

My enrollment at San Diego State University brought with it moments of eagerness, anxiety, and wonderful discoveries. There were many assignments to write, critical analysis to do and then more and more writing. Research and criticism of thought became the norm.

However, this did not completely erase the idea of escape into a better life from my mind. I would often take a break from the mental rigors of schoolwork to engage in sports, partying, activism and social movements.

This was especially so in my first year. But while they at first appeared to me as negative trends that threatened to derail my pursuit of academic success, I realized that they were in reality helping me tap into my inner being and guiding me to understand my calling in life.

I realized that through socializing it is important to make and keep friends in life because most of the people we socialize with become important entry points into various professional networks later in life. Friendships that are made in less formal settings make it easier to engage with influential people without having to go through the bureaucratic requirements of offices. It is these kinds of interactions that the modern day social media of FaceBook and Twitter have come to popularize.

Through my participation in activism and social movements, I came to appreciate myself more as a public speaker and as a champion for important causes that I believed in. These activities served as an important pedestal upon which my leadership skills were nurtured.

This realization came a little late, especially after I had posted poor grades on my transcripts for the first and second semesters in my first year. It took me a little more time to tame my newly discovered self and re-orient my energies towards the more important aspects of life.

Dissatisfied with the kind of grades I was getting, I decided to humble myself and look for help. I will never forget the assistance I got from Dr. Njubi Nesbitt, my professor of Political Science. The Kenyan-born scholar perfectly understood the kind of challenges I had been through and where I wanted to go in life. He took special interest in me and started inviting me to his office for discussions. He recommended the best reading materials and other academic resources; he did all he could to help improve my grades.

I recall Dr. Nesbitt doing something extraordinary to create opportunities just for me. In my second semester of my second year at the university, I was late to sign up for a course in African-American political thought. Knowing just how much this course meant to me, and wanting me to better understand African-American political and social ideas through critical examination of some of the major expressions of that discourse, Dr. Nesbitt made an exception to allow me and a few other students into his class, though it had registered full admission!

Since then, Dr. Nesbitt became an important part of my life—a mentor and a friend. As an accomplished scholar and given his roots in my region of origin, Dr. Nesbitt fully understood my strengths, my weaknesses, and the contexts within which my choices in life had been made.

At San Diego College, I had a chance to give a shot to my dream career. However, I had taken up a course in information and communications technology. At times I think this was a rebound from my not having made it in pharmacy, since I am not sure what I wanted to do with the associate degree in computers. I guess all I wanted at that level was any career that would help me stabilize in life—living just a cut above the dish washing fraternity.

It was at San Diego State University that I finally discovered my passion for public service and the desire to make a difference in people's lives. While at SDSU, I helped found the Somali Student Union. A main reason for this was the fact that there were several student unions specific to different groups, but Somalis lacked one they could closely identify with.

I felt that as Somalis, we needed a distinct identity just as we needed in high school, a banner under which we could meet and discuss matters that we felt were important to us. Furthermore, we needed to create a forum for mutual support, especially for new immigrants joining the university, as well as helping our members integrate better into the wider U.S. community.

When I first started gathering the requisite application materials to start the student organization, there was only one other student, Istarlin, who showed interest and commitment to the body. But I proceeded, and within a few weeks of launching the student body, the membership had garnered forty-four students from Somalia. The organization grew much bigger and is still in existence.

I completed my degree in Political Science in 2004. But my quest for education didn't end there. I have always wanted to continue learning and developing myself.

I still can't imagine how my life would have been had I not heeded my family's advice to keep pushing on no matter what. I must admit that there are many opportunities available for me now that I have earned degrees that are not available for many others who never pursued education. This is not a statement of pride or basking in self-glory, but a reflection of the regrets that many of my friends who never took the opportunity to pursue education express whenever we meet.

My quest to develop skills in leadership and management propelled me take up a Master's of Science degree in Leadership and Management. As I write this book, I am pursuing my doctorate in Public Administration at Hamline University in St. Paul, Minnesota. My course draws much from, and provides a convergence of thoughts in various disciplines, among them political science, economics, sociology and leadership studies. The knowledge that I am now seeking has practical application in public and private sectors, as well as in nongovernmental organizational settings.

This quest for more knowledge is informed by a simple discovery that I had made earlier. I had found out that a two-year Associate's degree or a four-year Bachelor's degree demonstrate a proficiency in the level of your education, but a Master's degree indicates a level of expertise in a specific area of study.

Looking back to where I have come from, I find great sense in the saying that the extent of your pain and suffering carves out a cup within you—the deeper your suffering, the deeper the cup. The size and space of this cup also represents one's capacity to experience love and joy. As deep as my suffering was during those years, so is my ability to feel joy and happiness in life in the present.

Like many of my compatriots in high school, I could have dropped out of school and made a living making minimum wage at best which would not make ends meet. That at times seemed as the easiest route. But I am glad I persevered in my pursuit of knowledge. Learning English was difficult and adapting to a new country on a new continent was not easy. On the contrary, getting an education was an imperative and not an option for my family. Therefore, I had to continue with learning and this is still what I am doing currently.

# Chapter 9
## Retracing the Steps
## In my Career Life

Getting a good job is often a dream come true, whether you live in America or any other part of the world. Let me put it this way, finding a well-paying job where you feel dignified and motivated to do more can be a very gratifying experience. This is more so considering the cut throat competition that exists even for the simplest of job opportunities that spring up.

In the current state of affairs, especially after the recent economic crisis in Greece, Spain and Portugal among other parts of Europe, as well as the Arab Spring revolution that recently swept across Tunisia, Egypt, Libya and Syria, coupled with the recession that hit the United States in the last several years, getting meaningful employment that caters for your family needs has become elusive for many.

But the dream lives on. The quest for a better life overshadows virtually any other desire in the modern American life. For instance, just like me, anyone would want to see his or her children go to better schools than he did, eat better and generally live life in an environment that is far much better than where he was brought up. This is the desire of every American, and the dream of every immigrant who crosses the ocean to come over here. Indeed it is the desire of each one of us.

But how often do new immigrants end up achieving this? How long does it take for them to settle down, find gainful employment or start a business and grow to the point that one can say they are stable? How many fresh immigrants ever get to the top in major organizations by advancing through the corporate hierarchy? And if they do, how long does it take?

It is tragic to note that, in the absence of good education and professional training, the majority of immigrants get ensnared in the rat race of having to do several menial jobs just to make ends meet.

Like I pointed out earlier, the majority of the certificates and diplomas that most immigrants hold are not recognized, and they have to start over again from scratch. One has to get professionally recognized certificates, degrees and diplomas to be licensed to practice his or her profession in the United States.

Unfortunately, this is a task that many immigrants find too expensive to undertake, considering that one has to work in order to earn a living. To get college fees, one has to take up several jobs, and get to the classroom either tired or worried about how to commute to the next duty station to make the extra dollar.

In this kind of life, frustrations grow by the day. It is more or less like trying to climb up a slippery hill. At times you feel like you're almost at the top and then suddenly something happens, and you're sent skidding all the way back to the bottom.

Essentially, most immigrants end up sacrificing their life just to ensure that their children get a better chance at life. The generation of adult immigrants who cross the ocean eventually realize that the best they can do under the circumstances they find themselves in, is to suspend the dream of comfort and affluence, and instead prioritize their children's education and professional growth. This is usually in the hope that the future will bring better tidings for the entire family; that is, at least once the children are well educated and have meaningful occupations.

I saw this in my family too. My elder siblings, with whom we came over, having no recognizable professional credentials to talk about, had to struggle with menial jobs just to get along. The first priority was getting us to school and making sure that we had most of what we required to see us through education.

So, if you're still in doubt, that's where we picked up life as a family upon coming to the United States. We started off in the rat race, whereby we had to do menial jobs to make ends meet. I too had to work at a McDonald's outlet in Denver, since the circumstances dictated so.

After talking to his boss about our family's financial woes, Wali managed to convince his boss that I needed to work over summer. So the hiring manager asked Wali to take me over to McDonald's  for the interview. Interestingly, I had zero interview skills, no previous work experience, I suffered from English language deficiency, and I completely lacked understanding of how recruitment processes work. All this stood in the way of my getting the job.

Nervous as I was, I went over for the scheduled interview. I took Wali's advice to simply respond to the specific questions asked and not try to give many explanations
or justifications. Hard as this was, Wali had asked me not
to demonstrate any signs of nervousness or desperation.
I did the best I could.

I cannot recall what the interviewer's name was, but
she was one of the most kind and welcoming ladies that I
had so far encountered in the U.S. Her questions seemed
quite easy, though I could not articulate proper responses due to my limited language knowledge.

"Why should we hire you?" she asked.

"Because I want to work hard," I responded.

"Are you looking for fulltime or part-time opportunity?"

"Yes."

"Your job will mainly involve cleaning utensils and assisting with food preparations. What do you expect to
earn?"

"A lot of money."

## Foundations of Professionalism

Saying that I was horrible on this interview would be an
understatement. I felt perhaps Wali should have given
me an idea of what to expect at the interview. I blamed
him for this, yet at the same time I couldn't help but regret having let him down completely. I felt that had I met
him on my way out, I would have apologized to him for
having me—an idiot—for a brother.

I recall the interviewer putting down her pen and
spring-bound A5 sized notebook, then proceeding in

a more relaxed discussion. This happened barely five minutes into the session. I felt embarrassed that there was nothing sensible coming from my mouth that was worth putting down, save for my name. Soon the subject had changed from a job interview to a counseling session on what to do if I hoped to make it through life in the United States.

"Hamse, in case—I am saying just in case because there's no certainty here—we grant you a chance to work, do not dream of making this your destiny. You're still young and full of life. Don't get scared of challenges that life brings your way—at least you have time on your side. Would you like to pursue education once schools reopen?"

"Yes," I replied.

Silence followed. I could see the lady was deep in thought. She pulled out the day's paper and started flipping through the pages as if searching for some specific information. Had I blown my chances? Was the lady so shocked that she lacked the right words to say to me? The silence was confounding!

The more I thought about this, the harder and louder I found myself cracking my knuckles. This was something I rarely ever did. Why was I doing all the wrong things today? I wondered.

"We will call you up in a few days and let you know about the next steps," she said after a few moments. That was the end of the interview. I stood up and reached for the doorknob with my left hand. I tried to turn the knob but my hand slid over the silvery metal and the lock noisily slid back into the hook on the door frame.

"Slowly, my dear," came the lady's voice.

Nervousness! I felt as though the lady wanted me out of the office pretty fast. But those were just my fears; she had indeed been very kind towards me. My hands were sweating profusely. I wiped them against my flanks, and then I tried the knob a second time with my right hand. It worked and I stepped out.

I felt like the world had fallen apart. I felt completely lost and emotionally drained. Yes, I deserved a pat on my back for having done such a thorough job of humiliating myself at my first ever job interview.

I found my way to the parking lot and waited for Wali's lunch break so he could drive me back home. At least I knew there would be peace at home, and no one would pass judgment on me.

I believe Wali must have done a great job at convincing his boss to hire me nonetheless, since I got it much to my surprise. Unlike her earlier promise, there wasn't any phone call informing me of my interview's performance. Rather, she just asked Wali to take me along for work orientation and other related requirements.

Although I have never asked Wali how I fared in the interview, I have come to believe the interview was just a formality.

The lady wanted to give me some means of sustenance, though she had to sound a tough to make me understand that the work place is a different world compared to what I might have been socialized to.

Consequently, I was taken in and after completing the basic training and passing the company's mandatory drugs test, I began my job.

Adapting to my new job at McDonalds wasn't difficult since my brothers were working there already. We would leave home together in the second hand family car that we had purchased and drive ourselves over to McDonalds. I was lucky too that I had Wali as my boss, at least for the first few weeks, and this gave me the chance to learn the ropes and develop the confidence I needed to execute my duties. I was earning $4.25 an hour.

There was no clear description of my job; I was supposed to do whatever general duties my seniors thought needed to be done. At one moment I would be scrubbing the floor, and the next moment I would be carrying the chefs' aprons from the changing rooms to the laundry section when shifts changed. But out of all the jobs I had to do, I felt most pathetic about washing dishes.

Not that I like dirty dishes—I would raise hell if I were ever served in utensils with traces of leftover food. I would feel nauseated too if I found out that any of my food was cooked in unclean utensils. I thus had to be meticulous, much as I loathed the job.

Although, when I think of it now, it's not the job that I hated, but its routine nature. Naturally, I like creative tasks that put my mental skills to test. On the contrary, this was not the case when it got to washing of dishes.

There was basically no creativity to dish washing except the tedium. No thinking was required, just back-breaking routines of sinking lidded boxes (used to keep lettuce and stuff in) in hot water, removing the lids and scraping off the leftovers. There were hundreds of squeegees and tongs to be cleaned, which would get pretty grubby.

There was a king-size Arch French Fry machine that had to be washed daily, sauce bottles and dressings, sauce guns, breakfast trolleys, removable work surfaces and the grilles on drink dispensers. The job was simply monotonous--more so given that there were customers streaming in and out virtually throughout the day. This meant that the monotonous ritual would not cease for the entire shift.

Lowly paying as the job might have been, it gave me invaluable culinary skills that I cherish to this day. For instance I learned how to make sandwiches and chicken nuggets. These are a favorite in my home and I like preparing them for my family over the weekends. I learned to follow the chefs and observed their tricks each time I had some free time.

My thinking was that should my dream of schooling get interrupted for any reason, at least I could seek apprenticeship in the kitchen. And maybe, just maybe, I would make a living out of preparing omelets, sandwiches and hot dogs.

Another good thing I carry with me to this day out of the experience is that it helped me appreciate the plight of the people such as cleaners and others in blue color jobs. Although many cleaning jobs are done with better equipment nowadays, I have learned to treat people in such occupations with the dignity they deserve. It made me appreciate too the importance of being diligent in whatever I put my hands to do, as failure might affect the lives of so many other people.

For instance, I learned that use of unclean serving utensils at a restaurant could easily result in food poisoning. This can in turn lead to expensive legal suits and reputational risks that can lead to the outlet's closure. This would mean that the jobs of so many innocent people would be at stake. If this were to happen at a massive scale, the local economy would falter.

I will forever remain grateful to McDonalds for exposing me to the American system of work, earning, and living. It inculcated into me the importance of working together as a team, adherence to professional ethics, as well as personal discipline. From observing the different roles that each one of us played in the kitchen, it made me understand better the meaning of the all too common analogy of cogs and gears at the workplace. Both are important in making a system run and none can function without the other. What's more, I learned the importance of not allowing personal emotions to take precedence in the work place.

I was lucky to witness a few unfortunate incidents for example one where an employee snapped at a colleague for inconsequential reasons. Digging a bit deeper, one would realize that the cause for this had absolutely nothing to do with the person suffering the tirade, but rather an incident that had taken place far away from the work place.

For instance, there was this middle-aged co-worker. Let me call him Jack, just to mask his identity since he is today a much more influential person in Denver's business circles.

On this day Jack reported to work late and was summoned to the supervisor's office so that he could give an explanation. As it turned out, this was not his first, second, or third warning for the same mistake, but somehow he had been let off the hook because of his hard work.

However, on this day he gave the supervisor a piece of his mind. To Jack, the supervisor was conspiring to have him fired, just as Jack's wife was working hard to divorce him and eject him from their matrimonial home on grounds that Jack was never home, but always at work. This was not withstanding the fact that Jack's shift always ended at 5 p.m. without extension, so no one knew where he spent the evening after work.

As the supervisor tried to explain to Jack that work policies needed to be respected, Jack descended on him with obscenities. He dared the supervisor to proceed with his plans to have him fired, and he would curse the day he became a supervisor.

We tried to intervene and contain the situation as a back office affair, but someone had already pressed the panic button and before we knew it, the police were already there. The two were taken in for questioning. Two days later, the supervisor was back to work, but Jack got fired.

As I grew older, this experience acquired a more relevant meaning in my life, especially more so when I got married and started a family. I discovered that even though I might have a busy job, I have to be there for my family. I have to take care of family issues and not allow small matters to get out of hand.

It is such unresolved matters that cause people to do crazy things they never thought they could ever do. A little nagging here and there, an unfulfilled promise, failure to apologize and such, can lead to bitterness, resentment and buildup of anger over time. In such situations, the slightest provocation can lead to actions with regrettable consequences. And as was the case with Jack, conflict with the supervisor didn't stop Jack's wife from proceeding with the divorce suit, neither did it solve any of the underlying issues in his family. It just compounded his problems.

Jack's experience aside, working at McDonalds reinforced in me the belief that without education, Hamse Warfa is nobody. Just how true could that be!

The job was not dignified at all. It is the kind of work you do while always being afraid of what issues the boss will pick on and the repercussions that will follow. No matter how well you work, you are always looking over your shoulders in fear of getting fired. It was not unusual to hear people snap, curse and even at times throw in the towel in resignation to fate.

However, those who quit were people who had lived longer in the United States, or those who had been born here. They knew their way around the city and they could get better deals elsewhere. But what would become of me? I had no skills or working experience with which to arm myself in search of another job. I was pretty young too and an immigrant. I just felt I needed to persevere, at least for the time being. Once I had learned the ropes, I would assert myself and resist being shoved around. So, in my heart I knew for sure life wasn't going to remain like that forever, at least not while I still had a chance at education.

It is these struggles that always brought back the reality that I was after all in school; so, I had to work hard.

I kept reassuring myself that my destiny wasn't in dish washing or packing foods for customers so that I could earn a pittance. I purposed to train my thoughts on higher value for my life. I thus saw my pursuit for education as an important escape from this kind of life.

**Yearning for Change**
My passion to work in the public service had started earlier in life, though somehow I never knew that it would turn out to be my career. I recall doing voluntary jobs in refugee camps at Dadaab and Utange. Much of what I had done then, in the company of a few friends, was to help new families move into the facilities, find space and set up structures and settle down. I also frequently queued for food rations, water and other supplies on behalf of elderly members of the refugee community at both camps, something that some of my age mates saw as thankless tasks.

However, a turning point that got me thinking more about venturing into public service came upon moving to San Diego, California.

Unlike in Denver where institutions functioned as they should and social support recipients were handled with much dignity, much of the public assistance we received at San Diego fell short of our expectations. This was perhaps on account of the huge immigrant population in San Diego. I still recall how humiliating it was in San Diego for a family to be recipients of welfare assistance, deserving as the situation might have been.

From my understanding, the purpose of any public assistance program should be to help the people get back on their own feet. It should be to provide short-term assistance in times of crisis, as opposed to perpetuating long-term dependence. During such times of need, families that depend on public assistance should be treated with the dignity that they deserve.

It is the poor service accorded to the needy families service without dignity–and the demeaning treatment we received at the welfare offices in San Diego that made me start thinking about what difference I could make in public service. I recall that our request for assistance was handled with utmost insensitivity to the extent that one day Mom almost broke down upon getting home from an unsuccessful attempt to secure help. I loved my Mom so much and I didn't like the look of frustration that was now developing on her face.

The process of seeking assistance turned into a long-drawn affliction, lasting over a month. The fact is that we needed assistance urgently because we were running out of essential supplies. Also, we needed medical insurance cards as soon as possible.

I remember how it had all began. My sister Fardowsa called the local Department of Human Services, only to get hung up on even before anyone had listened to her case. We couldn't believe it. Disgusting as it was, we decided to treat it as a technical hitch and tried to think of some excuses if only to reassure ourselves of our human dignity.

As a result, we resolved to visit the office in person the following day. Fardowsa, Abdirizak and I accompanied Mom to the offices in San Diego. After waiting in the queue for a couple of hours, we were served by a caseworker. The encounter lasted less than a minute. The caseworker gave us an appointment for two weeks down the line. There had not been any sensitivity shown for our needs, especially the urgent need for medical cards to get health checkups, more so at a time like this when Mom was struggling with her high blood pressure.

We returned home completely frustrated. Yes, this was America, but the treatment we had received on this day was no different from the indifference of camp administrators at times in Dadaab and Utange refugee camps back in Kenya, though not as severe.

Deep within I swore that if God ever gave me a chance to work with the needy, I would care enough to listen to their pleas and not just apply the same response template to every case. I would serve them as dignified people, I wouldn't allow stereotypes and blanket generalizations to cloud my judgment of who people are and their pleas for help.

The two weeks that followed felt like a century of waiting. We spent the little cash we had on us. We returned to the Department of Human Services as per our scheduled meeting. The agenda was to determine our eligibility to receive food stamps, medical and cash assistance. As we were not the only family being served, we sat in the waiting room for almost three-and-a-half hours. We could not eat or drink at the service's offices as bringing food and drinks to the premises was prohibited.

Finally we got to meet the same lady caseworker in her office. Once again she looked quite technical with everything she did—no human face in her service delivery. She had perhaps listened to cases far worse than ours, or the sheer volume and routine nature of the lady's work must have eaten up her heart. She was just there, seemingly immune to the plight of all the people that she was employed to serve. Without much ado, the strenuous interview process began.

She took our details once again as she had done the first time we had met. I felt it would have been easier for her to pull out the file from the shelf, but standing up was perhaps too much work for her.

We gave her every detail she needed and she put the information down in a new file. She didn't look up all the while, but kept mumbling the questions while looking down for the most part at the forms she was filling in.

One of the most chastening questions I recall Mom being asked was how much money she had in the house. She said she didn't have any—which was indeed true. We were thereafter certified eligible for public assistance.

This was to be the beginning of a long process of submitting monthly reports on whether any material changes had taken place at home, including whether we had a new child born, anyone had died, whether we received any cash, started work, left or started school among others.

After this humiliating experience of looking for social service we felt as a family, we were to do whatever we could to reclaim the family's dignity. We were to work at whatever job opportunity that presented itself.

As a way of reducing our reliance on social welfare, my brother Abdirizak and I found jobs as part-time security guards with a private security firm. We took up the job and did it zealously, knowing that our lives depended on it.

Working as a security officer was quite different from the role that I had played at McDonald's. Here, the job involved staying awake at night awaiting danger. Many are the nights I spent worrying about what would happen if the facility I was guarding got attacked, or if an employee cunningly sneaked valuables out. Needless to say, these kinds of fears were emotionally draining, something that was affecting my academic work.

But the job had to be done and Hamse and Abdirizak had to prop up the family financially. So each day after classes at 4:00 p.m., I would take up a completely new self. I would put on the security guard's uniform, hit the road to my duty station and remain standing till the end of my shift at midnight.

The facility I was employed to guard was about three miles from home. On the days when I didn't have enough money to pay for transport, I often got home at around 1:00 a.m., and still be expected to be in good shape by 6.30 a.m., when I would wake up an prepare to go to school. This is what we had to do for basic survival.

Three months into my role as a security officer, my sister Fardowsa started working at a retail store selling clothes. This brought the relief I had prayed for all along. I was at last free to focus on my schoolwork, which had become less of a priority in our struggle for survival.

But I was still not off the hook completely; I had to work for my own upkeep. And being unskilled, manual labor was my stable. I took up driving lessons in the evenings in the hope of landing some job. Upon completing the lessons and getting my driver's license, I got a part-time job as a cab driver at Avis Rental Car, earning minimum wages during summer.

Doing menial work was a tough kind of life that included doing insignificant jobs that hardly anyone appreciated. I was earning amounts less than could meet my needs, so how could I have saved to do anything significant in life? The jobs had taken away much of the time that I needed for assignments, revision and other academic pursuits. But rather than break me, this challenge seemed to strengthen my resolve to push on harder with education.

I reasoned that if I were to someday work in a big office impacting the lives of thousands in circumstances similar to those I had lived in, the only way was through rising beyond the circumstances. In other words, I had to fly above the weather if I ever hoped to create a vision of how life would be once the storm had passed. It's only from such heights that I could see miles ahead of the dark clouds.

To rise that high, I would have to build my capacity to articulate issues. I would need access to professional networks, much as I had a burning passion to help those in need. These were the factors that kept nudging me to push on further each day in my quest for education.

This vision is being actualized in a big way in my life. Through continued acquisition of knowledge and skills, I have been able to rise from a dish washer in Denver, as well as being a security officer and driver in San Diego. I do not give these examples to illustrate just how terrible some jobs can be, but rather to help you see how far a dream can carry one irrespective of how lowly we begin.

Otherwise, there is no problem being a dish washer if that's your chosen destiny. There isn't a thing wrong with being a guard, cab driver, ticketing officer or virtually any other job if that's your dream.

However, if you have higher dreams, never mind the present circumstances—I have been there long enough to understand that hard times don't last a lifetime. There isn't a night too long to defeat sunshine in the morning. Thus, do whatever it takes to legally and morally get yourself to your destiny without allowing the baggage of the past to bog you down.

## Scaling Higher Grounds

Minnesota had always been home away from home for me. My wife and I used to visit members of our extended family in the state at least four times a year. Given our growing network of friends and family already living in the state, we started exploring possibilities of relocating to join them. A golden opportunity finally came when I got a job as a Program Officer with Margaret Cargil Foundation in 2012. I moved over with my wife and kids.

My goal is to be a transformational leader and a public servant in the state of Minnesota, besides advocating for increased access to education for immigrants and low income families.

In the mean time, I still serve in the same capacity with the Foundation. I manage grants and work closely with organizations that assist communities to develop and implement projects in environmental conservation, aging, children and family services, arts and culture, health, and animal welfare. I also work with organizations that help communities recover and build resilience when affected by natural disasters.

This fits perfectly with my earlier vision for assisting those in need and helping them to rebuild their lives in a healthy and meaningful way. My passion is in helping others and nothing can stand in the way of this calling.

It lightens up my heart each time a proposal for funding lands on my desk for a project to uplift the living conditions of communities.

Prior to joining Margaret A. Cargill Philanthropies, I served as a Senior Program Officer at Alliance Healthcare Foundation. This is a San Diego-based organization working to improve access to healthcare for the underserved communities including refugees and immigrants and supporting organizations who address HIV, Mental health and substance abuse interventions.

In my capacity as a senior program officer, I managed community grants worth millions of dollars annually. I will forever remain grateful to God for the opportunity he gave me, first to go through the not-so-good experiences as a refugee in Africa, as a new immigrant in the United States, and later as a Senior Program Officer in an organization that sought to help those underserved in our society.

I felt that perhaps there wasn't a better person for the job than I was. From my previous experiences with life, I understand the meaning of deprivation and the cost of delayed service delivery to people in need. I understand the pain of being treated as a mere statistic. I thus did my duty as a Senior Program Officer joining the effort to provide access to health and healthcare for those underserved. It was a rewarding experience for me.

From 2001 to 2008, I was the Associate Executive Director for Horn of Africa, a nonprofit organization formed in 1995 to promote successful integration both physically and emotionally of the East African refugee population in San Diego.

I worked under Abdi Mohamoud, a man I respect for his commitment towards the betterment of his community. Abdi has been leading the organization since its foundation. The organization has over the years played a leading role in the integration of the Somali immigrant community in San Diego, now home to one of the largest Somali immigrant communities in the United States after Minnesota.

At Horn of Africa, I helped Abdi with the development and implementation of programs and organizational policies, including the hiring, training, support, as well as motivation and evaluation of staff. I helped supervise a team of fifteen staff members and twenty-six volunteers. In addition, as an ambassador for the organization, I often articulated the organization's goals and values to many constituencies, including foundations, state and federal agencies, community leaders and other public officials.

With the collaboration of my colleagues and the board, we developed the organization's strategic plan and promoted strategic alliances with other agencies and corporate partners to help the organization achieve its mandate.

I helped Horn of Africa develop and maintain partnerships that resulted in the successful implementation of collaborative program initiatives. On behalf of the organization, I also engaged community members from different ethnic backgrounds to get involved with the organization's work.

For instance, I engaged the San Diego Unified School District and formed partnership with the Race and Human Relations department of the district, worked collaboratively with the San Diego Multicultural Police, and successfully implemented various programs with many different nonprofit agencies.

My drive to see greater awareness of the immigrant community's ability to live better and meaningful lives saw me organize community based workshops on topics ranging from health and education to welfare and housing issues.

My work in the nonprofit sector has seen me serve in various volunteer-based leadership positions. One significant role was when I served as the chairperson for the San Diego Refugee Forum, a professional monthly round table bringing together organizations and advocates serving populations fleeing persecution and seeking refuge in San Diego. In this capacity, I worked closely with member resettlement organizations on how to better serve the community.

A major reason why I got so many opportunities to serve in such organizations is simply because of my passion for philanthropic work combined with the skills that I have and which the organizations were looking for. In order to move forward and propagate an important agenda, organizations seek for the most talented individuals that they can get; thus, they look for individuals with the right combination of aptitude and skills for the job.

Much of the success in my philanthropic work is owed to a Master of Science degree in Human Services with emphasis on Organizational Management and Leadership that I obtained in 2006. I acknowledge that the graduate courses prepared me well for organizational leadership.

Through leadership skills and strategic visioning skills I acquired in college, I was able to form and serve as first president of the Institute for Horn of Africa Studies and Affairs (IHASA). This is a think-tank that engages in research on socio-economic justice issues facing people in the Horn of Africa region and in the Diaspora. This gave me an important platform in public policy advocacy especially on issues touching on immigrants both nationally and internationally, and peace building.

But looking back at it all, I still feel that my work and commitment to improving the conditions for underserved and most vulnerable in our society irrespective of geographic location has just begun. I have come to appreciate that human needs keep growing in diversity and complexity, a major reason why society leaders and other actors need to keep engaging their people in debates on important policies and other issues affecting the society. I feel, much more than ever before, I want to have a lasting impact on my society and on humanity in general, wherever I will get the chance to serve.

# Part 5

# Leadership

# Chapter 10
# Rethinking Leadership

We all know of leaders who accomplished great feats for their people. These include Mohammed, Jesus, Buddha, and the Dalai Lama among others in the religious circles; Abraham Lincoln, Martin Luther King, Winston Churchill, Mahatma Gandhi and Nelson Mandela among others in political spheres; as well as the likes of Mother Teresa, Bono, Andrew Carnegie and Prince Karim Aga Khan IV in charity work.

The world is also full of leaders in media such as Ted Turner, Oprah Winfrey, Alton Brown, Annie Whitting ton and Barbara Walters among others, secular musicians such as Mariah Carey, Whitney Houston and Michael Jackson, and many more that would form volumes of their own were we to enumerate them. These people have had great impact on how the world thinks about the issues that they represent.

During the struggle for India's independence from British colonial rule in the 1940s, Mahatma Gandhi taught the world that there could be change without bloodshed. He came to be known for his opposition to violent revolution in dealing with the socio-economic and political issues in India.

Nelson Mandela, for his part showed the world the value of patience and long suffering. His twenty-seven years of incarceration first at Robben Island, and later in Pollsmoor Prison and Victor Verster Prison didn't deter his long cherished dream of seeing the state of South Africa free from apartheid rule.

In 1990, Mandela was set free, and out he came to lead the Africa National Congress (ANC) political party, which pressured President Frederik de Klerk to abolish apartheid rule. Mandela was to later get elected as the first black president of the modern day South Africa.

Mother Theresa taught the world the true meaning of self-sacrifice, human dignity, and the need to be mindful of the less fortunate among us—even those in their last moments in life. Born Albanian, Mother Teresa was to spend most of her adult life among the poorest populations in Calcutta in India.

While the rest of the world sought opportunities to make money, Mother Teresa started the Missionaries of Charity order in the Catholic Church to care for the "the hungry, the naked, the homeless, the crippled, the blind, the lepers, all those people who feel unwanted, unloved, uncared for throughout society, people that have become a burden to the society and are shunned by everyone," according to Mother Teresa's description.

Like most people, I have sought answers to the age-old question of what made these individuals, among others, great leaders. What extra faculties does, for instance, Barack Obama, Bill Clinton, Hillary Clinton, George Bush and other American leaders have that make them exceptional from the rest of us? Were these people born to be leaders or did they make deliberate efforts to achieve great leadership?

Does any ordinary boy or girl stand a chance at greatly influencing people and galvanizing their thoughts and energies towards a constructive course? And if so, what would be such a child's path to greatness?

Looking at Nelson Mandela, George W. Bush and Mahatma Gandhi's backgrounds, one can't help but notice that they came from powerful families. Mandela came from the Thebu Royal family in South Africa. Likewise, Mahatma Gandhi had been born to a senior governor in Bania, Gujarat in India. George W. Bush, on his part, is the son of a former American president—George H.W. Bush.

Are there any innate traits that make some people better leaders than others? Barack Obama is the son to of an African immigrant from Kenya, who came to America in search of further education, and an American mother. Both of Mother Teresa's parents came from Kosovo. Although Teresa's father is known to have engaged in politics back in the days, he passed away when Teresa was only eight years old.

As I write this book, Barack Obama is the president of the United States, a global superpower. In recognition of Mother Teresa's contribution to making this a better world, she was honored in 1979 with the much-coveted Nobel Peace Prize.

Were these two also born leaders, or did circumstances in their lives trigger a desire in them to bring about a different way of life, and is this what caught the attention of the globe in the process?

Can there be leadership away from public limelight, and if so, what then would be the proper position for the leader to exercise leadership—from the front, from within the people, or from behind? Every coin has two sides to it; hence, what would be the consequences of poor leadership in the peoples' lives?

Growing up in Mogadishu under the reign of Siyad Barre, we were taught that national heroes and leaders were specific great men, mostly army generals and government officials. These people were revered. They were often quoted as sources of "orders from above," and their word was law. There were songs composed in their praise and these songs were played over and over on the national radio so that everyone would know what these heroes were doing for our great nation—the state of Somalia. Indeed, we were made to believe that such men were in their position by right.

I was later to learn that these were people selected by the president on the basis of loyalty. Most of them had no recognizable ideological stand on important matters. They were Barre's sycophants, carefully selected to help entrench a sort of personality cult, presenting Barre as the nation's father, and the "heroes" as the wise men in whose counsel Barre ruled.

Siyad Barre had himself taken over power by force after overthrowing Somalia's second president, Abdirashid Ali Shermarke, in 1969. So, Barre was now a dictator ruling over the Democratic Republic of Somalia. Talk of contradictions! As I grew up and continued learning, I couldn't help but marvel at how easily and often people get duped or subdued into accepting poor leadership the world over. But as it were under Barre's rule, might was right and power was its own justification!

Although this thought did not consciously occupy my mind at this early stage of my life, the question of who a leader is came into focus in my political science class at the University of San Diego in California where I enrolled for leadership studies. This was especially after the study of the concept of power—the ability to make people do things they would otherwise not have done. The reason why the populace will obey a bad leader is because he has power over them. I came to learn too that no one can sit on your back unless you bend down.

I learned that in a democracy, people surrender their collective abilities and vest them in their elected leaders. So, the leaders exercise the powers that the public has voluntarily given them.

This means that the leadership can only wield power to the extent that the public has voluntarily surrendered, and within the parameters set out in law. Should the leadership exceed these limits, the leadership loses public support and thus the moral obligation to exercise authority. The people thus have the right to demand fresh elections to bring to power a more legitimate authority.

In a non-democratic set up (and there are many of them), the leadership ascends to power through means other than universal suffrage. Though there might be laws governing the extent to which the leadership can exercise power and authority, these limits may just remain in law, leaving the leadership to exercise powers at the leader's whims.

Such autocratic tendencies form the bedrock upon which the recent political uprisings in the Arab world were founded. The uprisings swept across the Arab states of Tunisia, Libya, spreading to Egypt and Syria. The effects of these have been bloodshed of innocent people, the collapse of public support systems, destruction of infrastructure and the driving down of the national economy. These are damages that later come to prove too costly for the affected nations. The effects spiral to neighboring states, which have to shoulder the heavy burden of hosting refugees. That is the price that nations pay for poor leadership.

But these were not the first instances of the public rising against their leaders. Somalia had been there before, though I must confess I was a bit young to understand. But now the various parts of the jigsaw puzzle were beginning to fall into place.

So, you mean the reason why Somali people had rejected Siyad Barre's leadership was due to his exercise of powers that the people had not voluntarily surrendered to him? Correct! Indeed, he had risen to power through undemocratic means—a military coup d'état.

Also, you mean the reason why Somali people took up arms against Barre's government was because they felt the government was misusing a monopoly of force that the populace had not willingly surrendered to the government? Great!

So, you mean the reason why there were often dangerous cracks within the national military was because some soldiers and commanders felt that Siyad Barre was asking them to do things they would ordinarily not have done, such as being sent to crush legitimate demands for accountability in Government? Sure! Did they feel that the president was exercising powers that he legally did not have, or powers that the public had not willingly vested on him? Precisely!

**Greater Political Awareness**

The study of political science was beginning to open up my understanding of situations, circumstances and their relationships to my life. I began to understand the relationship between power and leadership and the immense positive and negative effects they can have on the people over whom they are exercised. It was beginning to dawn on me that the reason my family and I came seeking asylum in a foreign country was because Siyad Barre's government back in Somalia had failed in demonstrating leadership and proper use of state power.

The struggle to oust Barre had been mainly factional without a common command center. The campaign was thus launched guerilla-style, much like fleas would attack a dog from all over the body. The dog eventually comes down but only for the fleas to realize that it is from the dog that they have been feeding, and none of them has any agreeable idea on what to do next. How else can one describe the leadership vacuum that engulfed Somalia with the fall of Barre?

The fall of Barre's Government had created a leadership gap in Mogadishu, whereby there was no one who could galvanize the support of all the forces that had fought off the bad governance. Among the militia groups leading the assault were the Somali Salvation Democratic Front (SSDF), United Somali Congress (USC), Somali National Movement (SNM), as well as Somali Patriotic Movement (SPM). Non-violent agitators for Barre's removal included Somali Democratic Movement (SDM), the Somali Democratic Alliance (SDA) and the Somali Manifesto Group (SMG).

Sadly, once the agenda of removing Barre from power had been accomplished, the various groups could hardly agree on the way forward for Somalia. What followed were showdowns, with respective groups hailing their own contribution to achieving the feat, thus staking a higher claim to power over other groups. The result was group rivalries, intra-group rivalries, and eventual continuation of armed conflicts, this time against the groups themselves.

Mogadishu became the most dangerous place on earth. Soon the war took clan dimensions, as the various factions were mainly based on clans. The end result of these conflicts was the loss of innocent lives including deliberate attacks because of clan affiliations, the displacement of populations, the destruction of property and infrastructure, and an entire generation born and raised in the battlefields.

These are the children of war who have never enjoyed the benefit of immunization from diseases such as polio, TB and measles. They have never seen the inside of a classroom, so they might never learn ethics or leadership. Their lifestyle has mainly revolved around playing soccer with AK 47 rifles tagged at their backs and shoulders. A few years from now these youth might be contesting for leadership positions in their country and they might get it!

The more I studied the concepts of power, authority, democracy and leadership, the more I felt I was getting to the root cause of the problem in my mother country, and the more I pitied the country's leadership for not having fixed the problem long before it had become a global shame.

Over the two decades that Somalia has experienced anarchy, I came to learn it was as a result of selfishness and short sightedness of leaders, sometimes warlords and powerful men with private armies whose only pre-occupation was capture and exercise of power—legally or otherwise. Sadly, these people have had such a tight grip on Somalia, and nothing can progress without their consent.

These private armies reigned terror on their own communities and levied exorbitant taxes to sustain their status as a public nuisance. Consequences for not remitting the taxes or for openly opposing their misrule were death. This is the kind of anarchy that spread beyond the country's legal borders and into the Indian Ocean in form of piracy.

The pirates would waylay ships passing through the Gulf of Aden, take them over by force and demand ransom for the release of the vessels, cargo and crew. The ransoms would run into millions of dollars per year, part of which would be used in acquiring even more sophisticated assault equipment from the black market, and the remaining amount would be handed over to the lords of anarchy to do as they pleased. Until recently, the international community was busy focusing on treating the symptom of the piracy problem by coming up with temporary security measures rather than helping Somalis build an effective federal government with strong institutions including the implementation of new federal constitution.

It has been these same warlords in Somalia who have over the past two decades played a critical role in scuttling efforts aimed at establishing peace and proper governance in the country, as that would mean an end to their wicked lifestyles. However, the most painful thing to note is that such lifestyles have been sustained at the expense of national growth, and at the expense of the future of Somali people.

It is this kind of thought that makes me feel that Somalia, of all nations of the world, has paid the most painful price and for much too long, for poor leadership. If my dream of helping out my people would ever come true, it would start with fixing the real problem—leadership.

I love Somalia, and I have always wished to be part of the team that will one day bring lasting peace to my country of origin. Now that I had placed my finger right at the heart of Somalia's woes, what was I supposed to do next? I knew that I couldn't give what I never had. I had to first seek to develop myself into the change that I wanted to see in Somalia. Now that leadership was the problem, I had to train to be a good leader and seek to help and mold more Somalis, both in the U.S., in Somalia, around the Horn of Africa region and in the Diaspora into proper leaders. I felt the urgency of the matter—the change had to start with me!

I vowed to study, understand and internalize leadership skills, wherever that quest led me. I knew that it was by first understanding the concepts of leadership and power that I would be in a position to impact and promote good leadership back at home as well as in the U.S. This was going to enable me to help the communities that I got the chance to work for or work with.

I have since discovered that the best leaders in every situation—in the family, learning institutions, work place and even nationally—are made, not born. I have come to discover too, out of my interactions with leaders and people involved in developing leadership in various institutions, that the desire to lead comes from within. In other words, one must have a vision and the self-drive to see things in a different and better way, and hence move to create a similar vision among the people. It is this desire to create a better way of life that leads one to seek further training on how to best articulate the leadership vision and make it real for the people.

In the quest for deeper understanding of politics, I came to realize the close link that exists between leadership and economics. You can't lead hungry people unless you have a solution to their hunger. People will only follow you if there is something in it for them—so leadership is about people, showing them a way towards solutions to their problems. In solving the problems, you also achieve a strategic end for yourself however you may define the end. This is what they call a win-win situation. Leadership is about putting others first.

This discovery was a real eye opener into the character of leaders across the world. Without mentioning names, I am sure you already know of leaders who are elected on a platform of ending public miseries such as lack of economic opportunities, poor living conditions, ending corruption and many such promises.

Once they get into power, the leaders quickly abandon the thought of solving the problems, fearing that in the next elections he or she would not have a campaign plat-form on which to contest. As a result, the leader makes calculations of the kind of problems to solve, and which ones to entrench further, so that he can talk of complet-ing the development projects he had started during the last electoral term.

I have seen the cost and impact of poor leadership on the masses. These people would otherwise have had their problems solved and their potential unlocked in a fraction of time. Unfortunately, this is never actualized and the resources are squandered and job creation ends up being a mirage.

We have corporations being led by managers trained in some of the best universities in the world, but the cor-porations' performance still falters. We have organiza-tions headed by leaders trained in the best institutions in the world, yet they still under perform. Why? Is there a fusion of management and leadership that needs to be infused into modern organizations?

Contrary to my earlier thoughts, leadership is a much more complex issue than I had always imagined. While I thought a master's degree would be sufficient to help me understand the real depths of what ails our society, I must now appreciate that the more one studies, the more uncertain things become. The more you learn the more you discover things you should have known much ear-lier, things you should be getting aware of right as you read, as well as things you need to know in your quest to move forward. It can at times feel overwhelming.

This notwithstanding, I was resolute that I needed all the leadership aptitudes that life has to offer to help make not only Somalia, but the world, a better place. This quest for knowledge has not ended as yet. I am currently pursuing my doctorate in Public Administration, encompassing leadership, political science, economics and related fields.

One of the most important lessons that I have learned is that anyone can become a leader if he or she really wants to be one. This is irrespective of one's parentage, upbringing, life's challenges or whatever hurdles stand in one's path. Leadership is for the willing and the resolute. It is the aspiration for those creative enough to dream of a better way of life, a better solution to the problems facing the society.

I have learned too that there are people who should have been leaders but they shied away for one reason or another. There can't be a better definition of timidity than this—running in the opposite direction when life and society call you up to show the way. Isn't it true that a major reason why we have so many failures in leadership is because someone abdicated? Bad things happen when good people fail to stand up for what is good, and so the unprepared take over!

## Mitigating Leadership Needs
Although one can be a well-trained leader, one's discharge of duty or exercise of responsibilities can be influenced by his or her personality. I have seen people

become better leaders when their belief systems, values and ethics, come to reinforce the skills learned in class.

Mother Teresa's belief in the dignity of the human soul led her to do what most other missionaries would have thought twice before engaging in. Though a Catholic by religion, her acts and strong personality saw her being given a temple dedicated to a Hindu god to convert it into a hospice. This is the kind of impartial leadership that the world is crying for today.

I have seen great leaders who for one reason or the other turned disastrous because of their inability to shed off their stereotypical perception of other people's cultures, religions and gender. It is such shackles that make some leaders look down upon their subjects, sections of their subjects, or even opponents in a contest. Think of people such as Pol Pot in Cambodia and Augusto Pinochet in Chile. These, among other callous leaders across the world, have only set themselves up as examples of bad leadership.

Many people who would have otherwise remained bystanders in the journey of life have come to become influential and inspirational leaders the world over through their desire for change and proper training in leadership. They sought solutions to important problems and out of their obscurity they emerged to become significant players in global agendas. In this context I can't help but think of the late Professor Wangari Maathai.

The recipient of the 2004 Nobel Peace Prize and the first African woman recipient of the same was a trained Veterinary Doctor who decried the rampant destruction of the environment in Kenya. She chose not to stand aside and watch as the very institutions, including the nation's presidency, that were supposed to be custodians of national good resort to bringing down forests and the country's water towers.

The founder of the Green Belt Movement, Professor Wangari Maathai's battles with law enforcers under president Daniel Moi, who was protecting the very people destroying key indigenous forests, among them Karura forest in the outskirts of Kenya's capital, Nairobi, are well documented.

Through these bold steps, a woman who would have perhaps spent her life treating sick animals grew into a global leader on matters of environmental protection.

I have come to appreciate the subtle fact that the majority of the leaders are people we will never hear of in public. These are simple people like you and me, who continue making small incrementally influential decisions to carry forth our dreams one day at a time. Surprisingly, this is where majority of the world's greatest leaders are found.

Think of a mother who, though not educated herself, encourages her child to go to school each morning. She might not herself be well off or even be considered a leader in the community but she envisions a better life for the child and inspires the child to push on, one day at a time. To me, that is true leadership.

We are all leaders in our own rights. We make important decisions regarding our own lives and those of others all the time, but we hardly ever shout about it from the rooftops. We are intelligent enough to see the future we want for ourselves and the people around us, yet local enough to remain among our people, making clear the vision and encouraging them to make that essential step towards the dream.

Realizing that I didn't have to be of a certain pedigree to be a good leader, I vowed to start exercising leadership skills right from where I was.

In 2004, the relationship between the San Diego Unified School District and the local Somali community was at its worst, thanks to the periodic in-school and street fights pitting Somali and African American youths. While the local African American communities saw Somalis as unwanted intruders, Somalis were looking to the local authorities to help them begin life in a peaceful country.

The authorities, on their part, had not been keen to draw a line between the African Americans and the Somalis. The two parties were, in the eyes of the authorities, one and the same violent lot! As a result there was little assistance given. In school, Somali kids felt they were being discriminated against.

Sensing a leadership vacuum, a number of community leaders and I stepped forward and helped establish the Somali-district committee, which became a key organ in the resolution of many conflicts. The committee also helped create better understanding between the Somali community and the local San Diego School District, which resulted in better treatment of Somali kids in school.

The organ also played a key role in creating harmony between the local African American community and the Somalis, significantly reducing the fights that had become all too common in the area.

In scholarly circles, there had been strong feelings that most of the scholars writing about East African affairs, politics and conflicts, were mainly foreigners. Many African scholars had felt that some of these foreign-directed studies and writings—some of which were already being cited by East Africa Scholars—were representing the facts on the ground as seen from their (the scholars') foreign ideological lenses, and not necessarily as the reality on the ground.

This resulted in misconceptions and misrepresentations of the dynamics of East African politics, economics and development, especially in the western world. As an East African, such misrepresentations actually hurt me, as it did many other scholars from the region. I felt that the time had come to rectify the situation. This came with the formation of the Institute of Horn of Africa Studies and Affairs (IHASA) in 2008. This is the think tank that engages in research and policy work both in the Diaspora and in the Horn of Africa region.

The formation of this institute came from my strong belief that knowledge is a socially constructed phenomenon. As such, our "knowledge" or "center of gravity" as East Africans could be different based on our local understanding of the situations and circumstances we live in. As a result, I was making an attempt to create a body of knowledge sourced from the grass roots level. Such a feat required focused and decisive leadership, and I am glad I rose up to the occasion and provided the solution.

Today, IHASA brings together thousands of East African and foreign-based scholars with an interest in the Horn of Africa region in annual congress to discuss, to exchange knowledge and ideas, and to network. The institute has been influential in shaping thoughts and discourses on social, economic and political issues regarding the horn of Africa region, with a view to building good governance, reducing violence, bringing about development for the communities and encouraging economic integration in the region.

It is through IHASA that I came to meet a wonderful man who helped broker peace between Ethiopia and Eritrea in the 1990s. His name is Charles "Chic" Dambach, a recently retired chief of staff for Congressman John Garamendi and former president and CEO of the Alliance for Peace Building, which I recently joined as a board member.

Chic has helped establish networks of organizations and professionals to help create peace and security worldwide. This great soldier of peace was to become my mentor, and it is he who introduced me to the concept of peace building (in fact, he helped establish the universally accepted definition of peacebuilding and he has promoted the concept of building peace, as well as use of the term worldwide). He has come to be a great personal friend and a resource for IHASA.

Since completing advanced training in conflict analysis and resolution from the U.S. Institute of Peace, I took up the challenge to provide free workshops to youth, focusing on conflict analysis training, conflict resolution, and teaching the importance of advocating for peace. I am to this day very passionate about this role, given the devastating effects of war that caused us to come here as immigrants.

I have devoted a lot of my energy, resources and leadership to peace building initiatives through IHASA. We have partnered with among other think tanks: the Woodrow Wilson Center and Alliance for Peace Building to promote regional peace in the Horn of Africa region. IHASA's work is triggering bigger impact and broader regional change in analyzing and working with ways that prevent or reduce conflicts. Another area we have been making good progress in is transitional justice. The focus is on empowering Somali women to have greater say in national issues. Such voices are often missing in decision-making processes.

We are looking at creating wider access to the "xeer" system as a dispute resolution platform, especially in rural Somalia. Essentially, xeer is a traditional Somali legal system, where elders serve as judges and help mediate cases using precedents. This customary law system has been a subject of study by many modern scholars. The centuries old system has especially been identified as an important aspect of social development within the conflict-prone Somalia. Here, we have been looking at creating wider acceptance of women voices in the traditional justice system.

Since its formation in 2008, IHASA has become one of the leading think tanks on issues regarding the Horn of Africa. The institute publishes reports on the state of peace and development in the region. The body has given me a number of important links, including my connections to key elected officials and their congressional staff. I have been called up a few times for congressional briefings.

As an immigrant to the United States, I was privy to the fact that a number of asylum seekers from East Africa would often not know of the next step once they got to the United States. For this reason, the majority of them found their way into jails, bundled up together with hard core criminals. Even after one's innocence had been proven, most of the immigrants would feel disoriented and disillusioned with the American life, thanks to the rude reception they had received.

This was not the right kind of treatment for such people. They needed to be received well. When they did wrong, they deserved to be heard and accorded proper dignity. They were, after all, looking for a better life, just like millions of other nationals who come to the United States. Feeling the need for advocacy for their plight, I became one of the first responders who sought legal services to help out the asylum seekers. Most of the legal assistance comes from law firms offering pro-bono services. This has been instrumental in representing these people's cases in the quest to rebuild their lives in the United States. This was a need clearly calling for leadership, and I am glad I helped fill the gap along with many other community leaders. I cannot forget the continued assistance most asylum seekers received from Survivors of Torture International, a San Diego-based nonprofit organization that provides an array of services including healing for those who are victims of torture in their native countries.

Above all, I am glad that I have been able to demonstrate solid leadership in my professional life. Joining Horn of Africa, the organization's leadership recognized my potential and promoted me to the position of Associate Executive Director.

**Leadership in Organizations**

Joining Alliance Healthcare Foundation in 2008, I started off in a position of leadership, serving as a Program Officer managing grants worth millions of dollars. At that level, I defined leadership as an inward drive for myself and others.

In my career in nonprofit organizations, I have come to appreciate that being assigned a role above your colleagues does not necessarily make you a good leader. It simply makes you the boss. Bosses are associated with exercise of authority, something also known as assigned leadership.

True leadership is demonstrated when you begin to inspire your team to perform better toward the stated goals. This is what scholars refer to as emergent leadership. In other words, being assigned a job title isn't in itself recognition of leadership; it is what you do with the position—inspiring the people to deliver—that defines you as a leader.

When dealing with communities in need of assistance, I have always sensed deep within how much the individuals' desire that I, on behalf of my organization, will demonstrate understanding and sensitivity to their plight. It is said that a society's values can be gauged by how it treats the weakest in their midst.

A more significant leadership role that I often played at Alliance for Healthcare Foundation was representing the foundation in community activities and by partnering with other organizations and persons who were addressing community needs. Through demonstration of leadership skills, I was promoted to Senior Program Officer.

In 2012, I joined Margaret A. Cargill Philanthropies as a Program Officer to manage strategic grants that fall outside of our defined sub-plans but still fit within our mission and vision. Here, I work closely with the Vice President of programs and other senior leadership to providing meaningful support to society at the community level.

Working closely my foundation's leadership and others earlier in my career has taught me fundamental lessons about organizational leadership. There can't be effective leadership without proper communication, for it is through communication—both talking and listening—that a leader wins the trust of the people. A key part of my work has thus been communicating with my colleagues internally, as well as with program implementation partners, to create the best possible understanding of the objectives that we have set out to achieve. In this way, I have seen both internal and external partners develop higher levels of confidence in their work. I have learned that there can't be a better way of positively inspiring staff than listening to their ideas of how they wish to contribute to the organization's growth.

I have come to appreciate the impact that sharing information on organizational plans can have as a motivator to the staff. I get excited each time the vice-president or our foundation's trustees provide organizational updates or information on certain programs we funded and the impact they have had on the ground. It gives me a sense of purpose in my work and a satisfaction that runs deep in my heart. This is the type of work that I would love to see myself doing even if I got a message that the organization has no money to compensate us and we had to wait a year or so, I would do so without a complaint.

I have come to appreciate that good leadership creates a sense of ownership of processes–be it at home, at work or nationally. It inspires people to contribute more towards the advancement of a common course, which improves their lives and that of others. I have come to discover, too, that contrary to what most people in leadership think; poor exercise of power and authority almost always has worse consequences than what is actually seen at face value. Much of the mess left behind by such leaders leaves a life-long impact on their people.

# Chapter 11
## Lessons From My Life

Looking back at the entire experience since my childhood, I am grateful to God that He chose that to be my path in life. This acceptance has helped me accept the many things that I could not change, and has also renewed my resolve to take charge of what I can change for the better.

Despite my determination and that of my fellow twenty neighborhood kids to take the message of peace to the war generals in Mogadishu, Somalia, truth is that there was nothing we could have done to stop the conflict. As I came to realize much later, the war was not about us - the kids - it was about matters more complex than we could comprehend at that age.

The troubles that both sides—the government and the opposition forces—were grappling with were too weighty to be resolved with antiwar slogans from poor little kids. Proof to this is the fact that even the United States and the U.N. moved in to help but finally pulled out of the country three years later after it was clear that no solution was forthcoming. The war dragged on for over two decades.

This has taught me that as I journey through life, I will encounter many situations that I might never be able to change despite the best of my efforts. At times there will be storms that will be too powerful even for the entire U.S. Government with its technological sophistication to hold back or avert. The best thing I can do about such is to either avoid them if I can, or find a way to lessen their impact on my life.

## Lesson in Corporate Strategy

Our escape from Mogadishu was such an emotional time for my family and me. It was hard leaving the only place I called home, and this coming after I had lost some of my closest friends to the war brought with it some of the lowest moments in life.

But from that experience I can today draw an important lesson on corporate strategy. Dad loved us so much, but I guess he had been over-optimistic that the armed conflicts wouldn't reach our neighborhood. For that reason we delayed the escape till our neighbor's home was hit. I have never wanted to imagine what the outcome would have been had the fire gone off target and hit our home.

This is a common blunder made by many leaders, including sharp brains in corporate America. You can see a problem approaching or an ugly situation developing around your life, business or job. But for the simple reason that such has never happened to you before, you assume it won't affect you.

This reminds me of a corporation such as Kodak, whose leadership saw the advent of digital photography approaching, but remained over-optimistic that the digital imaging revolution wouldn't affect the huge investments that the company had made in previous technologies. When reality finally hit home, it was too late for Kodak's captains to steer the ship off the icebergs' course.

The same lesson applies to other aspects of life and of career planning as well. You could be in a career line or job position, yet all signs point to possible termination. But for the simple fact that you have never been sacked before, you believe the oncoming restructuring won't affect you. So, you continue burying your head in the sand till you realize your back is on fire!

I've learned to study circumstances objectively, and to weigh the possible impact of my decisions on myself and many other people who might be depending on me directly or indirectly.

**Seeing the Silver Lining**

Hard times have taught me how to see the positive side of the struggles. Mogadishu was such a great place before the war. But many a times I ask myself: "Who or what would I have become had I remained in the city all my life?"

There are high chances that I would perhaps not have gotten as good of an education and mentorship in leadership as I got here in the U.S. Maybe my life would have revolved around fetching livestock from herders in Somali's vast grasslands for export to Qatar and Yemen. That is not to diminish the value of the kind of life that Somalis live or the importance of the livestock export business to Somali's national economy, but in a personal capacity, I perhaps wouldn't have lived to the fullness of my potential.

Isn't it true that most people learn the value of love after they've lost an important person in their lives? That's what happened to me after losing my father during my early teenage life. As Joe Nichols says in his song "The Impossible," "Sometimes the things you thought could never happen just like that!" The pain of losing my father was almost unbearable, but it helped me to cherish my mother, sisters, brothers, and everyone else around me even more, knowing that we won't be on earth forever. It also made me appreciate the value of relationships.

**Teamwork and Purpose**

The senseless destruction of lives and livelihoods that we experienced in Somalia was a direct consequence of an ill-executed strategy. Do not get me wrong; the motive was perfect and legitimate, but the strategy side of it is the hole through which the water leaked in and sank the entire ship.

Truth is that President Siyad Barre had been a dictator who dealt mercilessly with any dissenting voices. In many instances, it was alleged that he instructed his forces to execute people that he believed were opposed to his rule, and many times sent Special Forces to deal with entire communities which he suspected backed opposition elements.

However, the opposition approached his ouster without a concrete strategy of what to do or a commonly accepted governance structure to replace Siad Barre's regime. Thus, with ouster of Siad Barre came a power vacuum that the opposition leaders found hard to fill. As such, the victory ushered in unprecedented divisions among the opposition, with each faction laying claim to the victory, hence the mandate to rule the country. And that's where things got worse, and the civil war once again engulfed the entire country.

From this, I have learned that successful teamwork demands clarity of purpose and total commitment to the course for all the parties involved. It also calls for clear rules of engagement, proper definition of success, as well as clear direction on what will follow once the victory has been achieved. For instance, to the opposition forces in Somalia, success might have been defined as ouster of Siad Barre, but it is clear what followed was a prolonged civil conflict. This was an anti-climax that lasted more than two long decades.

Finally, I believe any team must have a functional system for conflict management and resolution. In the absence of this, every party might be tempted to pull towards one's own side and in the process tear apart the road map to success as happened with Somali's leadership after Siyad Barre.

## Continuous Personal Development

After experiencing the transformational power of a good education, I am today a firm believer that continuous learning is an important key to personal growth. For me, it has also been the key to financial freedom, as well as the means with which I hope to achieve most of the goals that I consider important in life.

Much of the zeal I have today to learn came from something that my father always reminded us back at home in Somalia. He told us that education is the key to life. Though he was not himself much learned, he was careful to point us in the right direction. He always cautioned us that even should he leave us his livestock export business, we would eventually bring it down unless we went to school to learn how to manage it.

At that young age I couldn't draw a link between education and success in life. None of the academic disciplines we learned in school taught us how to export livestock to the Middle East, so just how was education going to help me improve the family business?

Knowledge is not an end in itself, but rather a means to an end. Knowledge acquisition is an investment that comes at a price, but it will eventually prove the most valuable investment you ever made.

### Setbacks and Escapism

Sometimes a setback will be necessary to help you focus on what is most important in your life. Had I not suffered the serious ankle injury while at Crawford's High School, I would have perhaps continued in my escapism from the real challenge facing my life: the language barrier. However, being off the basketball court gave me the opportunity to reflect on my academic life and vow to make a difference.

Looking at your own life, could there be some truths that you've been seeking to run away from? Some people resort to drinking to escape the reality that their family life is not as great as it should be. Likewise, we have youths engaging in drugs to escape from the reality that success in life demands a little more effort than the youths are willing to put in.

I am sure you've tried to escape from reality, but will you wait until you suffer a misfortune to bring you back to where you're supposed to be? You don't have to! Leadership begins with taking charge of personal issues. It is all about gathering the courage to face and solve the issues you're grappling with before setting out to solve the global economic crisis.

## Nothing Can Outlast Persistence

There isn't a problem big enough to defeat your determination. With determination you can conquer even what you consider the biggest obstacle to your progress, be it in your personal, social or career life.

Much of the encouragement that I got from my family while I studied at Crawford High School made me see just how possible it was to bring down the Goliath of my language barrier. It took effort and persistence. I must admit I spent more time in the library and I bothered my teachers a bit more, but my persistence only ignited my family's and teachers' desire to help me more. It is this support that kindled my flame even through stormy times. Eventually, I conquered the language barrier, and this opened to me a whole new world of opportunities. It helped improve my grades and also restored my self-confidence.

So, what is it that you're almost giving up on? Is it quest for better performance at your work? Could it be a spouse or child who almost conquered their wayward behavior but then slipped back even deeper than where they were at the beginning? Is it quest for promotion that has over the years proved elusive, and you resolved to just sit back and await your fate?

Success still awaits you. Breakthrough is just around the corner. But only if you're willing to rise up again and give it another try—this time with conviction of victory.

## Some Career Paths Aren't Straight

Rebound decisions can be expensive and time consuming, and they might not yield the results you hoped for. Forgive me for coming up with this point, but well, it's the plain truth.

The main reason why I proceeded to study computer and information systems after high school was not because I fancied the course at all. It was simply a fallback from not having qualified for a bachelor's course in pharmacy. This is a common issue with people who are still undecided on what career to pursue. In most cases the decisions are not well evaluated and so they hardly align with one's lifetime goals and ambitions.

Is it a surprise therefore, that we have so many highly trained professionals earning decent salaries but nonetheless wishing they were in a different career? That's where I almost ended up, were it not for moments of deep soul searching. In the end, I figured out that I wanted to deal more with helping those in need. Undoubtedly, this had been impacted by my experiences of hunger and deprivation when growing up, and by seeing the emergency services delivered by people who had little concern for the recipients.

This is what got me into studying political science. Later on I took up a master's degree in management and leadership, and I am currently in pursuit of a doctorate in public administration. From all this I have discovered that doing something you like offers greater satisfaction than what money can buy. And the beauty of it all lies in the fact that by doing what falls along your line of passion, you no longer chase money, it is money that comes after you. You will have more people willing to pay you to do for them what you like doing, since you will do it much better than people doing it for the money.

## Great Leadership Starts With You

Most of us think of leaders as a unique class of people with special characteristics, which the rest of us lack. Coming to America, I didn't have the convincing kind of language to appeal to others. I didn't have the necessary articulation either. After all I was an immigrant, what new did I have to tell the natives whose grandparents were born, walked on and were buried on American soil?

However, life's circumstances have taught me that leadership isn't necessarily an inborn characteristic. Rather, it comes about by first identifying a need right where you are and availing yourself to help the people meet that need.

Opportunities for leadership keep springing up right where we are, we never really need to look far for chances to exercise leadership. Search first within where you are, and you will find enough such openings to keep you engaged for a lifetime. I have come to also appreciate the beauty of training as a way of enhancing one's leadership abilities. Though one might have come from a family where one or both of the parents happened to be leaders, this however, doesn't necessarily make one a good leader.

In order to best understand leadership and to apply the concepts in appropriate context and for best results, I would recommend some level of formal training in leadership. I say this because I have been a lay teacher as well as a trained leader, and I have experienced the difference that leadership training can create in a person.

## More Heights to Climb

Ultimately, I feel that even as I work to complete my doctoral studies in public administration at Hamline University, a whole new chapter is just about to open in my life. This is more so with the return to peace in my home country of Somalia, the formation of a new government, and the adoption of an interim constitution that features federalism as a key pillar of governance.

I strongly believe that full implementation of the interim constitution will present the people of Somalia with the best opportunity to rebuild the state. The new administrative structure will ensure fair representation of the people at regional and national levels, as well as equitable distribution of national resources. Such are exciting developments, as they present the country with the best opportunity at ending the hitherto existing strong sentiments of exclusion of some clans from national issues.

These are important developments that I would be proud to be part of, no matter the distance between the

United States and Somalia. I will thus be seeking to play a more significant role in national reconciliation, reconstruction and in the political, social and economic empowerment of Somalia's youth and women. I feel that there can't be a greater gift that the world can give to the people of Somalia than helping them to once again take full charge of their own lives. I know this won't be an easy thing to do, but I want to contribute my two-cents as a Somali-American to help in charting the way forward to an ever brighter future for the children of Somalia and the entire East Africa.

# Acknowledgements

While the story of my life evolves with each tick of the clock, I am excited to have you hold this copy of *America Here I Come: A Refugee's Quest for Hope*. Writing this book has been a great experience and an eye-opener for me. It has helped me put many things into their proper context in life, and has greatly contributed to my understanding of myself and the people around me better.

Writing this book would not have been possible without the contribution, guidance and mentoring that I have received from a number of people, some of whom I will mention below.

To start with, I would like to thank God for blessing me with such a great family. I specifically single out my beautiful wife, Ikran Abdi, for the continued motivation and encouragement that she has all along given me to write the story of my life. Ikran carried much of the family's responsibilities while I was in the basement working on this book.

I would also wish to thank my mother, Hindisa Seed, as well as all my brothers and sisters for being such great sources of inspiration. Special thanks go to Wali, Nasra,

Fardowsa, Hani, Kowsar, Abdirizak, my nephew Omar Warfa and my nieces Idil and Ismahan, for having availed themselves on countless occasions when I needed their assistance in stitching together the sequence of events as they happened in our earlier days in Mogadishu, in Kenya and upon coming to the United States.

While I had all along harbored the dream of authoring a book, I must acknowledge that the dream was catalyzed by Nancy Jamison, Executive Director of San Diego GrantMakers. Nancy introduced me to Marji Wilkens, who included my story in *The Try*, a book about ordinary Americans who had accomplished extraordinary things through personal perseverance.

I would thus wish to thank Nancy and Marji Wilkens, as well as Jim Owen, the author of *The Try*, for their individual and collective roles in creating the current demand for this full version of my story. Judy Bernstein, an accomplished author and great mentor, I can't thank you enough for the great coaching that you have given me about writing, and asking for absolutely nothing in return for your investment in my success.

There are many more wonderful people who without their assistance this book would not have been possible. These include John Wanjora for the many hours he worked with me in putting the story together, polishing the manuscript and the final editing. Ms. Anne Ehrhardt Wilbur, Dr. Larry Ndivo and Dr. Lidwien Kapteijns also spent countless hours editing the various versions of the manuscript and gave invaluable advice on how to improve the book. Anne Wayman, Patti Frazee and Scott Edelstein, all accomplished authors, gave their time to help me succeed in this book project. I also would like thank Matt Mussel, Agin Shaheed, Mohamed Hassan, Abdi Mohamoud, Francis Njubi Nesbitt, Hodan Hassan, and to all those who provided me their support.

It is difficult to quantify and pay back the enormous contributions in form of time and professional skills that all the above and other persons that I have not listed here have invested in this book. I thus wish to express my extreme appreciation for all they have done for me to realize my vision of publishing a book that will contribute positively to the ongoing discourse of the challenges that immigrant communities, especially those from my native region of the Horn of Africa, face upon coming to the United States.

Finally, to all those who have over the years helped me grow into who I am today, I can't thank you enough for your love, care and compassion.